PHILLY WAR ZONE

PHILLY WAR ZONE

Growing Up in a Racial Battleground

Kevin Purcell

Library of Congress Control Number:		2011914463
ISBN:	Hardcover	978-1-4653-5079-4
	Softcover	978-1-4653-5078-7
	Ebook	978-1-4653-5080-0

This book was printed in the United States of America.

To order additional copies of this book, contact:
Xlibris Corporation
1-888-795-4274
www.Xlibris.com
Orders@Xlibris.com
90746

WHY I WROTE THIS

When friends today ask me where I grew up, I tell them I grew up in a row home in Southwest Philly. Many then ask, "What was it like?" I tell them, "It was the greatest neighborhood a kid could grow up in, until I was 10. Then it began to turn into a racial battleground."

Some then ask me to tell them more. To which I usually reply, "It's a long story," and leave it at that.

Well, this is my long story.

I finally got my chance to put my story into words – thanks, in large part, to The Great Recession of 2008. The recession brought my advertising business to a virtual standstill. So I used that time to write the only long story I've ever wanted to tell.

This is my account of events that stand out in my mind from the four most dangerous years of my life: starting in 1969, when I was 10, and ending in 1973, when I was 14. I've tried to tell my story as I would have as a 14-year-old, just three days before my family was finally, through a near-miracle, able to move to a safer neighborhood.

Please don't get me wrong. I have many more happy memories than dangerous memories of my childhood. But the dangerous memories – including two kids stabbed to death in gang-related violence – have lingered in my mind for years. So, in that respect, it's been somewhat therapeutic to recall the details of those dangerous times. All the events in this book are true. Most names and a lot of details have been changed to respect the privacy of those involved.

In a sense, my story is more than just a story about our Southwest Philly neighborhood. My story takes place around the time of the civil rights movement, when racial tension was high throughout the country. As black people demanded the same rights as white people, race riots were breaking out in cities nationwide, including a big riot in North Philly in 1964. During this time of racial unrest, many stories just like mine were unfolding as kids like us, black and white, from working-class neighborhoods suddenly found ourselves on the front lines of upheaval.

As dangerous as our neighborhood was, I realize it in no way compares to some of the all-but-hopeless neighborhoods so many people in this country and around the world are stuck living in today, with no relief in sight. The more I see their images on TV and read about them in the newspaper, the more my heart goes out to those people.

I dedicate this book to my wife, Jeani, and our two children, Christian and Jenny-kate, who have provided me with the best years of my life. But this book must also be dedicated to all the guys who "had my back" during the most dangerous years of my life.

Thanks for your interest in my story.

ACKNOWLEDGMENTS

Foremost, I'd like to thank my wife, Jeani, for tirelessly taking time to read through so many of my 51 drafts of this book. Her patience was endless, and her feedback was constantly insightful. I'd also like to thank my children, Christian and Jenny-kate, for all their support and understanding during the countless hours I've spent putting this book together.

Special thanks also goes to three literary professionals who guided me through the process of writing my first book. Thanks to Cynthia Maniglia, my former advertising colleague; Dr. Hal Gullan, prolific author; and Brad Fisher, longtime book editor, for allowing me to tap into their vast experience.

I'd also like to thank Paul Gillam for his design work on the cover photography, the cover layout, and the map of our old neighborhood. I'd like to thank Bill Dorsch, a friend from our old neighborhood, for allowing me to use his photographs. Finally, I'd like to thank all the employees at Temple University's Urban Archives, who were so helpful every time I stopped by to do more research for my book.

If you'd like to comment on the book, you can post your thoughts on Facebook at Philly War Zone, or you can email me directly at: phillywarzone@aol.com.

CONTENTS

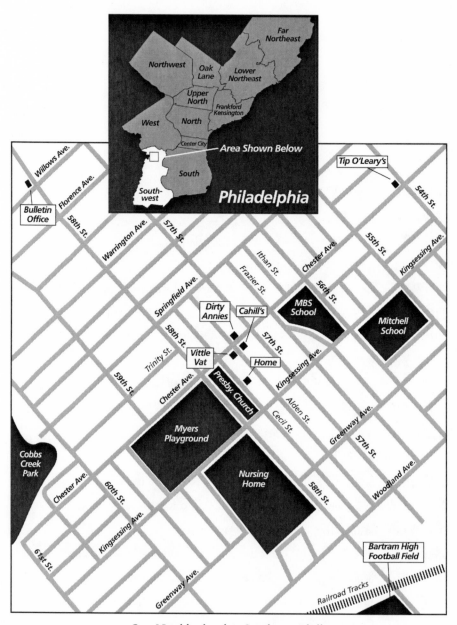

Our Neighborhood in Southwest Philly

CHAPTER 1
June 6, 1973:
Only Three More Days

THE SECOND I *step off the trolley at 57th and Chester Avenue, they jump out from behind a parked beer truck and surround me. This time there are three of them.*

"Honky mother-fucker, let's see how tough you are today," says Willie, the strongest of the three. I know from experience Willie's the strongest. His punches hurt like hell.

Ever since the weather started getting warmer, these three black kids and some of their friends have been waiting for me two or three times a week on my way home from high school. They know where I live. And they know I get off this trolley by myself every afternoon around four o'clock.

I never started any shit with any of these guys. They want to kick my ass just because I'm in one of the only white gangs left in our neighborhood in Southwest Philly, a neighborhood that's become a racial battleground these past few years.

"Alright," I say, "I'll fight you, Willie … just me and you." I learned from one of the older guys in the neighborhood that, whenever I'm outnumbered, I should always offer to fight the toughest-looking guy. He says it'll make them think I'm a little crazy. Today, I ain't fighting any of them. The last time I tried to have a fair fight with Willie, I was winning the fight at first. Then the other two guys started punching me from the sides, and I found myself trying to defend myself against all three of them. They punched me around pretty good,

especially Willie, until they saw a cop car coming and took off running. I ain't making that same mistake today.

As I lean over to put my three hard-cover schoolbooks on the sidewalk, I quickly yank them back up in front of my face and bulldoze my way past the smallest of the three kids. Then I dart out between parked cars and make a quick right, running side-by-side in the same direction with passing cars, waiting for a break in traffic so I can cut across Chester Avenue. Thank God I'm fast. As dangerous as this neighborhood is now, if I weren't fast, I wouldn't be able to get away from these kinds of situations nearly as often as I do.

I finally see the opening in traffic I've been waiting for, so I quickly cut across Chester Avenue. When I look back, I see the three black kids are still coming after me, no surprise there. I keep running toward my house, just a half-block away on Cecil Street, the farthest of two small streets between 57th Street and 58th Street. As soon as I get to the first small street, Alden Street, I look up. Oh shit, I'm trapped. Another black kid is up ahead near Cecil Street, waiting for me. He's one of Willie's friends, the tall, thin kid who always has a metal hair pick sticking out from the side of his huge afro. Nearly every black kid my age has an afro, but this kid's afro is huge, almost as big as Dr. J's afro.

"We got you now, mother-fucker," he says as he runs toward me. I've only got one option. I cut left up Alden Street, then I make a quick right into the back alley that leads to Cecil Street. I could run up the center alley toward my backyard, but the barking dogs remind me of the nasty German Shepherd I'd have to run by. That dog is mean, and he's big, so big his head easily stretches over his backyard's wrought-iron fence into the narrow alley. Last time I ran by him, he almost bit my left ear. Besides, even if I run up the center alley and jump into my backyard, I won't be able to get in our back door. We always keep it double-bolted shut.

So I keep running straight ahead toward the Cecil Street end of the alley, knowing that the kid with the hair pick in his afro is probably circling back on Chester Avenue to get to the same spot before I do. So it's basically a footrace between me and him, and he's got a lot less distance to cover. This is going to be close.

If only I had my car antenna with me. It's my favorite weapon for situations like this. But I can't bring my car antenna to school with me. Even worse, I'm not even wearing my belt with the thick buckle, my second favorite weapon. Today, I'm wearing these new, green bell-bottoms Mom bought me that don't have loops for a belt.

I keep running as fast as I can. When I look up, there he is. The kid with the big afro got to the end of the alley before I did. Even so, I have no choice but to keep running straight at him. The only other thing I could do is turn back and run at the three guys chasing me from behind. *That wouldn't be smart. At least I've still got my schoolbooks. I'll use them as a shield again and try to plow right through him. I've also got to be ready in case he tries to use his metal hair pick as a weapon.* My friend Chris got stabbed in the head with a hair pick a couple months ago and had to get four stitches to close the cut. As I get closer and closer to the conflict to come, I do what I always do in situations like this. I quietly begin to pray, "Our Father, Who art in Heaven ..." as I run as fast as I can to build up some momentum for the collision ahead.

Then something really weird happens. The kid who's waiting for me at the end of the alley suddenly turns and walks away. *I'm totally confused now. I have no idea what's going on, but I have to keep running.* The other three guys are still chasing me from behind.

Right on! Up ahead, I now see the best sight my eyes could see. A shiny blue cop car is stopped at the end of the alley where the kid had been waiting for me. *I'm still not used to the blue cop cars.* Philly cop cars were red my whole life until a couple of years earlier, when Rizzo became mayor and had all the cop cars painted blue.

Now that I see the cop car, it all makes sense. When the black kid saw the cop driving down Cecil Street, he turned and walked away like nothing was happening. The cop in the car is looking out the passenger window directly into the alley to see what's going on. I keep running toward the cop car as I point behind me with the thumb of my right hand so the cop will see the three kids chasing me. Evidently, one of the kids sees the cop, too.

I hear him yell, "Cop. There's a cop. Turn around."

I glance back and see the three of them are turning around and heading back to the Alden Street end of the alley. As I run out of the alley onto Cecil Street, the cop car quickly pulls away and makes a sharp right turn onto Chester Avenue to try to catch the kids who were chasing me. *I hope he catches them.*

Now I can finally relax. I stop running and try to catch my breath as I walk the final 50 yards to our tiny, two-story row home where I live with my parents and four brothers.

Why do they have to start shit with me all the time? I think to myself. *I've never started a fight with any of them. I just wish everybody could get along.* But I know it's well beyond that point now. In the past couple years, this neighborhood has become one of the most dangerous places in all of Philly. In just the past 10 months, two young kids – one black and one white – have been stabbed to death. The white kid was a couple years older than me, but I knew him pretty well. We played basketball together for years. Just minutes before *he was killed, he was part of our group walking home together after a night of playing basketball.*

Thank God we're finally moving out of this neighborhood on Saturday. I only have to deal with this shit for three more days. I was beginning to think we'd never be able to move out. But thanks to a near-miracle, it's finally happening, and Saturday can't come fast enough.

Just a few years ago, this was the greatest neighborhood a kid my age could grow up in. Like any neighborhood, ours had its share of kids who liked to start trouble. But I can't imagine any neighborhood being more fun and safe to grow up in. Back then, on a warm June afternoon like today, I didn't have a care in the world. Around this time of day, I'd be taking my time walking home with my friends from Most Blessed Sacrament School, or "MBS" as everyone called it. Once home, I'd quickly get out of my school clothes, put on my play clothes, and be on my way to my favorite place in the world, Myers playground.

Myers playground is just a half-block from our house, and it used to be the perfect place to hang out. Me and my brothers, Joe and Larry, were at Myers playground every day. The playground, which used to be an orphanage, takes up most of the two blocks between 58th Street and 60th Street, from Kingsessing Avenue to Chester Avenue.

Once I'd get to Myers playground, I'd get right into a game, any game, and keep on playing until dark. We played basketball, football, baseball, box-ball, sock-it-out, stick-ball, half-ball, wall-ball, and street hockey. We played one game after another all day long. At night, we'd watch the games in the playground's summer basketball leagues. Every summer, a lot of the best high school and college players in Philly played in those leagues. A few nights each summer, the playground workers would set up a movie projector outside and show a movie against the wall of one of the playground's three large, stone buildings. Lots of parents and kids would sit on blankets and lawn chairs to watch the movie. Every day, all day, there was something fun to do at Myers playground.

Most nights, we had to be back from the playground just after dark, but we didn't have to go in yet. So we'd round up all the kids from the Cecil Street area and play games like "Ring-up" and "Hide-the-Belt" for at least another hour. No matter what game we were playing, the game came to an immediate stop the moment we heard the bell ringing from the water-ice truck. The truck was about the size of a bread truck, white with round edges. The truck would drive down Cecil Street and stop about halfway down the street, just past our house. All us kids and lots of parents would line up to buy water ice and soft pretzels. Then we'd all sit on the front steps and eat away. I liked to wait until my chocolate water ice began to melt, then I'd dip my soft pretzel into the melted, chocolate-flavored ice. I can still taste it just thinking about it.

I always felt so safe on Cecil Street. On warm summer nights, lots of adults would sit on soft cushions on the top step of the four concrete steps that led from the edge of our front porches down to the sidewalk. Neighbors would sit out for hours, talking with other neighbors, many of them enjoying a cold beer or some other cold drink. At least one neighbor would have the Phillies game blasting on their transistor radio. So we'd be able to keep track of the Phillies game while we were running up and down the street having fun. I knew everybody on Cecil Street, and they all knew me. In fact, I knew almost everybody in our section of the neighborhood. And I felt safe no matter where I went. All us kids knew that most parents around here looked out for all the kids, not just their own.

And there were kids everywhere. We lived in a mostly Irish-Catholic neighborhood that was packed with kids. There are five boys in our family, but we were considered a small family. Lots of families had eight, 10, 12 kids or more. Some of the really big families had to eat their meals in shifts because there wasn't enough room in their row homes for everyone to sit down to eat at the same time.

Our house on Cecil Street. From left: Marty, Larry, me, and Joe. Steven was still an infant.

So many kids lived in our neighborhood that MBS was one of the most crowded elementary schools in the country. When I started school at MBS in 1964, there were 101 kids in my first-grade classroom. There were 10 rows of 10 kids. The extra kid sat at a desk in a corner in the front of the classroom. To keep 101 kids under control, the rather large Catholic nun who was my first-grade teacher would walk up and down one row after another, tapping a wooden yardstick against her empty hand. We were all afraid of her, and we all knew she was eventually coming our way.

My classroom was not the only first-grade classroom with at least 100 kids. There were five more classrooms of first graders every bit as crowded as mine. At that time, MBS had nearly 3,500 kids from first grade through eighth grade. I always heard people say that MBS, back then, was the largest parochial school in the world. I'm 14 now, and I still don't know what the word "parochial" means, but, believe me, there were literally tons of kids.

So much has changed since then. So many white families have moved out of our neighborhood that MBS now has less than 1,200 kids. As more and more white families moved out, more and more black families moved in. These days, we can't even set foot in Myers playground anymore. Every time we try, we get attacked by black kids who now outnumber us by a lot. They don't want us in Myers playground anymore. In fact, they don't even want us in the neighborhood anymore. Problem is, we still live here.

I try to never leave my house without some kind of protection. First, I make sure I wear my belt with the thick buckle, except when I wear these new, green pants that don't have loops for a belt. I don't need to wear a belt. I've got a big butt that keeps my pants up without a belt. The only reason I wear a belt is because it's a great weapon, and it's perfectly legal. Plus, whenever I'm wearing my green Army coat, or anything else with long sleeves, I grab the metal car antenna that I hide in the tiny, three-foot-by-six-foot garden in the front of our house.

I found my car antenna lying in the street in front of our house a couple weeks ago. One of the older white guys must have left it there after a street fight. The older white guys hang out in a tough gang called the "Dirty Annies." They hang out right around the corner from my house. Lots of nights they get into street fights directly in front of our house. Me and my brothers watch a lot of their fights from our front window.

My car antenna is definitely my favorite weapon. I wish I could take it with me everywhere. It folds down to about 10 inches long, so it fits perfectly up my sleeve between my wrist and elbow. I walk right past cops with it up my sleeve all the time. Whenever black kids mess with me, I pull it out and it quickly extends to about three feet long. Just one swing creates enough room to give me a running start, and a better chance to get away. Plus, if I ever lose my antenna, I can easily get a new one by just snapping one off any car in the neighborhood, except some of those newer cars that have antennas with springs on the bottom. I wouldn't be surprised if they invented those springs to protect car antennas from young kids like us.

Nowadays, whenever I walk down my street, I have to be extra careful when I get close to the alley. Alleys in our neighborhood are very narrow, wide enough for just one person to walk through at a time. So it's hard to see if anyone's hiding in the alley until I'm right next to it. By then, it's too late. I learned that the hard way about a year ago when three black kids who were hiding in the alley tried to jump me. Good thing I had my car antenna with me that day. When I swung it a few times, the kids backed off, giving me just enough space to sprint back up Cecil Street and into my house. Since then, whenever I get close to an alley, I walk a few feet into the street until I pass it.

And these days, I never turn a corner until I peek around it first. I have to see if there are any black kids hanging out around the corner, and who they are. If I see any of the black kids who like to start shit, I go back and take the alley until I pass the area where they're hanging out. There are only two times I feel safe on the streets in this neighborhood: when cops are around (thank God, they're everywhere these days!) and when I finally meet up with my friends.

Today, it looks like I'll make it home untouched. Tomorrow, I might not be so lucky. Fortunately, I've only got to deal with this shit for three more days. In just three more days, I hope to start living the life of a normal 14-year-old in a normal neighborhood, like this neighborhood used to be before it started turning into a war zone.

CHAPTER 2
June, 1969:
"Hand Over Your Sneaks"

THE FIRST WEEK after school lets out was always my favorite week of the year: no more alarm clocks to wake up to, no more homework to do, and three months of non-stop fun at Myers playground to look forward to. So when I woke up on Monday morning of my first week with no school, the last thing on my mind was the trouble that lay ahead. The only thing on my mind was that today was the day I was getting new sneaks.

I definitely needed new sneaks. For more than a week, I'd been plugging up holes on the bottoms of both sneaks with cardboard packaging from Dad's dry-cleaned shirts. The bottom of my left sneaker showed more cardboard than rubber.

At about nine o'clock in the morning, I jumped down from my top bunk bed. I wanted to get my new sneaks early so I could play in them that afternoon. The first thing I did was try to wake my brother Joe, who was still asleep in the bunk below.

"Joe, c'mon, get up," I said as I gave him a nudge.

"Leave me alone. I wanna sleep," he mumbled.

"C'mon, get up," I said. "Let's get our sneaks early so we can play in 'em today."

"I don't care. I wanna sleep," he said.

"Fine," I said, "I'll go wake Larry up, and come back for you."

My brother Joe was 11 years old. I was 10. And my brother Larry was nine.

We might as well have all been the same age. We did everything together. Sure, we had our share of brotherly battles. But the three of us were really close. When I finally got Larry and Joe out of bed, we wolfed down a Pop Tart, drank an Instant Breakfast, and off we went to get our new sneaks.

Every boy in the neighborhood wanted to wear just one kind of sneaks: Converse All Stars. All the popular kids in the neighborhood wore them. Even most of the college basketball players on the Philly Big Five teams wore them. Our family couldn't afford them. Converse All Stars cost eight dollars and 50 cents for just one pair. Even though Dad was working two jobs, I could see that my parents didn't have a lot of money. I often overheard Mom and Dad talking about not having enough money to pay all the bills. There was no way they could afford eight dollars and 50 cents for one pair of sneakers, not the way we wore out our sneaks in the summer. We'd be lucky if we could get through a month without needing a new pair. So every time we needed new sneaks, Mom would take us on a four-block walk to a discount store called Tip O'Leary's. Tip O'Leary's sold sneaks called John Smiths that looked just like Converse All Stars, but they only cost three dollars a pair. The only visible difference between John Smiths and Converse All Stars was the label on both outside ankles. So as soon as we'd get home, we'd peel the labels off. Then our John Smiths looked just like Converse All Stars whose labels had fallen off. And that was good enough for me and my brothers.

My parents with their five boys in our Converse
look-a-like sneaks outside our cousins' house.

Tip O'Leary's store was near the corner of 54th and Chester Avenue. To get there, we'd walk along Chester Avenue past MBS Rectory, past MBS Church, and past all the stores along Chester Avenue between 56th Street and 54th Street, the area where most people in our neighborhood shopped. Along the way, we passed the real shoe store with real Converse All Stars in the window. We passed the store that sold all kinds of gag toys like fake vomit, whoopee cushions, smoke bombs, and hand buzzers. We passed the bank, the five-and-10-cent store, the bakery, the clothes store, the butcher shop, the drug store, the restaurant. About 40 stores in all lined the shopping area along both sides of Chester Avenue.

As we got closer to Tip O'Leary's, we passed where the old movie theater used to be. The movie theater closed down when I was about four or five years old. Ever since, whenever we wanted to see a movie, we had to walk eight blocks to 63rd and Woodland Avenue where there were two movie theaters on the same block. I'd recently been to one of those theaters to see *Planet of the Apes*. That was a cool movie; those apes looked so real.

Next to where the old movie theater used to be was a new supermarket. It was the first really big supermarket in our neighborhood, but it was too far from our house for us to shop there. We still shopped at two corner grocery stores near our home. When we walked past the supermarket, I saw a few black people mixed in with all the white people who were shopping. I never used to see black people in this area. But now the area near 54th Street was one of the first parts of our neighborhood where a lot of white families were moving out, and a lot of black families were moving in. Two of my friends from MBS who lived in this area moved out last year. Both of their families moved to the suburbs. And both of their houses were bought by black families.

Once in a while, I'd hear about fights breaking out in the 54th Street area between black kids and white kids. But all the stories I heard involved older teenagers. I figured kids our age had nothing to worry about. So as we made our way to Tip O'Leary's, our only care in the world was hoping we could find John Smith sneaks in our size.

At Tip O'Leary's, nobody measured our feet like they did at the real shoe store. We'd just dig through big plastic bins full of sneaks tied together in pairs, searching for a pair in our size. That day, all three of us found a pair that fit. When it was our turn to pay, Joe handed over the 10-dollar bill Mom had given him. He got one dollar back in change, and we walked out of the store, each of us carrying a bag with our brand-new sneaks.

The second we set foot outside Tip O'Leary's store, we were surrounded by six or seven black kids who were a lot bigger and older than we were. A couple of them looked about 13 or 14 years old.

The biggest kid said, "Hand over your sneaks, all y'all."

I was stunned. We were actually being robbed. I had no idea what to do. I looked over at my brother Joe, who was definitely a lot crazier than me and Larry. Joe lifted his bag up toward the kids as if he was going to hand his sneaks over. Then he swung the bag toward the faces of two of the black kids and yelled, "Run!"

And run we did. The three of us sprinted down Chester Avenue toward 55th Street. As we were running, I could see there were still lots of people out shopping up ahead. If we can make it to 55th Street, I thought to myself, we'll be safe. When we got to 55th Street, I looked back. Sure enough, the kids had stopped chasing us.

"Damn, that was close," I said to Joe and Larry, still trying to catch my breath.

"Nice move back there, Joe," Larry said.

"Hey, there ain't no way anyone's gettin' my new sneaks," Joe said. And he meant it.

Joe wasn't afraid of anything. He would fight anybody, no matter how big they were. And Joe wasn't much bigger than me or Larry. The three of us were all about average height and weight for kids nine, 10, and 11 years old. Me and Larry got into our share of fights, too. But we didn't get into nearly as many fights as Joe.

On our walk home from Tip O'Leary's, I kept seeing those guys trying to rob us over and over again in my mind. And every time, it was just as scary. I decided right then and there I was not going back to the 54th Street area any time soon. When we got home, we told Mom what happened. She wanted to call the cops. We tried to convince her not to. She finally agreed, saying, "Okay, but you're not going over to 54th Street again without me or Dad."

Mom was definitely the boss in our family. Because Dad was working two jobs, Mom had to take charge. And she became very good at it. Mom has always been as loving a mother as anyone could ever have. She always put all of our needs ahead of hers. It seemed like her entire life was centered around taking care of Dad and her five boys. But Mom was also tough. She watched us like a hawk. And whenever we messed up, she let us know about it right then and there, often with a hard slap, no matter where we were or who was watching.

Here's a perfect example. Whenever Mom heard one of us curse, she'd give us a quick slap to the face, and then, while wagging her index finger in our face, she'd say, "I'm gonna wash your dirty mouth out when we get home." And she would. She'd force a bar of soap into our mouths and keep it in there for a few seconds. The times she did it to me, I couldn't get that awful soapy taste out of my mouth for the rest of the day. So I always tried to make sure I didn't curse around Mom.

Mom was born in South Philly, near 15th and Reed Street. Both her parents were born in Italy. Mom's dad died when she was 10. After that, her mom had to work full-time in a factory in South Philly, making uniforms for the soldiers who were fighting in World War II. So Mom and her only brother had to live in an orphanage run by Catholic nuns. Mom always talked about how much she loved some of those nuns. She still kept in touch with a few of them. But there were also a couple nuns Mom didn't like so much. She said they were very tough on her and her brother. I often thought Mom's personality combined those two traits; she was an extremely loving mom who was tough as nails when she had to be.

Dad was definitely *not* the boss in our family. He was as easy-going as can be. Dad was from Philly, too. Mom and Dad met at a bar down the shore in Wildwood, New Jersey on Fourth-of-July weekend. The bar was called The Shamrock. Mom told me she didn't usually hang out in bars. Mom wasn't a drinker. She might have two or three drinks a year, tops, usually during the holidays. Mom said it was raining so hard that Fourth-of-July weekend that she and her girlfriends decided to go check out some bars. Dad was already in the bar with his twin brother, Uncle John. It's kind of ironic, but both of my parents were twins. Mom's twin died at birth. Anyway, Dad and Uncle John were in the Shamrock Bar, sitting near the front door, when Mom and her girlfriends walked in. Uncle John pretended he was the bouncer and asked to see the girls' ID cards. Dad and Uncle John ended up having a few drinks with the girls. Dad asked Mom out on a date. And the rest is history.

Dad grew up in West Philly, on 46th Street near Westminster Avenue. Both of Dad's parents were born in Ireland. Dad's mom died when he was seven. From everything I've heard, Dad and his four brothers were pretty much raised by their only sister, who was the oldest in the family. Dad's father was usually working. He delivered big blocks of dry ice to homes back in the days before everybody had refrigerators.

Because Dad had to work so much, he liked to spend as much free time as possible with us five boys. He really liked watching sports with us on TV, especially Big Five college basketball and the Phillies, Dad's favorite team. Many weekends, Dad would take all five of us to Cobbs Creek Park, a huge park that was about a half-mile away from our house. Dad would find some open space in the park where he'd teach us how to hit and field a baseball. Other times, Dad would take us to Myers playground to teach us how to play basketball. Dad loved basketball, and he was a great shooter. When Dad was in high school at St. Thomas More in West Philly, he once won the school's foul-shooting contest. Dad was such a good shooter that, one night at the Jersey shore, Dad was banned from the basketball-shooting game on Wildwood's boardwalk. They banned him when they noticed Dad's friends were paying him to shoot so he could win them some cigarettes. Dad told us that, back then, cigarettes were the most popular boardwalk prize for teenagers.

Dad's youngest brother, Uncle Jim, was the best basketball player in Dad's family. He played college basketball for St. Joe's, one of Philly's Big Five teams. Uncle Jim was now the basketball coach at Cardinal O'Hara High School in the suburbs. When I was younger, Uncle Jim used to coach at St. Thomas More High School. One of Uncle Jim's teams at St. Tommy More won the Catholic League Championship in 1961. I was too young to remember that. In 1968, Uncle Jim's Cardinal O'Hara team also won the Catholic League Championship. I'll never forget that. That championship game against Father Judge High School was the best comeback I'd ever seen in my life. Uncle Jim's team was losing by 13 points with two minutes and 18 seconds left in the game. Then Uncle Jim's team scored 13 points in a row, sent the game into overtime, and won the championship by one point in overtime!

I felt so proud when I'd read about Uncle Jim's team in the newspaper. Some of the articles even included his picture. A few years later, I would be just as proud reading about another basketball coach named Purcell. My Aunt Delores, Uncle John's wife, coached the girl's team at West Catholic High School to the 1970 Catholic League Championship.

Uncle Jim's incredible championship game was played at the Palestra on the University of Pennsylvania campus. The Palestra was usually the home court for all the Philly Big Five teams: Penn, St. Joe's, Temple, Villanova, and LaSalle. A lot of Saturday nights we'd take the "13" trolley to the Palestra to watch two Big Five games back-to-back. We were lucky that the Palestra was just a trolley ride away. Walking into the Palestra was like walking into a basketball museum: so much history, the scene of so many great Big Five games, the way the bleachers go straight up so everyone's close to the action. It felt like the game of basketball was invented to be played in the Palestra.

The only other place that gave me the same goose bumps I got walking into the Palestra was Connie Mack Stadium up in North Philly, where the Phillies used to play. I remember going there many times with our little league baseball teams. After our long bus ride up to North Philly, we'd have to wait in a huge line that practically circled the entire stadium, which was smack in the middle of a busy, inner-city neighborhood. After our long wait in line, we'd have to climb up flight after flight of narrow stairs. Then we'd follow our coaches around the stadium hallway to our section. And then, finally, we'd walk out to our seats. The moment I saw the grass field, the bright lights, and all the Phillies players I watched on TV all the time, I could feel my eyes opening as wide as they possibly could, trying to take it all in. It took my breath away. The long bus ride, the waiting in lines, the flights of stairs, it was all worth it and then some. And that's the same way I felt every time I laid eyes on the Palestra's basketball court. I was in awe.

Usually, when Dad took us to see Uncle Jim's basketball team play, we had to travel out to Cardinal O'Hara High School in the suburbs. Because we didn't have a car, we'd take a bus, an el, and another bus. On the way, I'd stare out the bus window, looking at all the big houses we'd pass by. I figured people who lived out in those big houses with those big yards must have an awful lot of money.

Like I was saying, Dad was as soft-spoken and easy-going as could be. He always wanted everything to go smoothly. He tried to like everybody and hoped everybody liked him. Even the few times Dad got mad, he was still soft-hearted. Dad would sometimes get upset when me, Joe, and Larry would be upstairs, jumping around and wrestling in the back bedroom. At that time, our favorite TV show was *Batman*. Mom had recently bought us the Batman record with the theme song from the TV show. So we'd put the record on the turntable and the three of us would take our places, each in a different corner of the back bedroom, waiting for the theme song to start. As soon as the song started, we'd attack each other, jumping off the bureau and the bunk bed onto the twin bed below, pretending to fight each other the way Batman and Robin fought the bad guys at the start of each show. After a few minutes of us jumping around in the bedroom, Dad would yell up from the bottom of the stairs, telling us to stop. If we didn't stop, and we usually didn't, Dad would come up with the belt. As soon as he came into the bedroom, the three of us would jump into the bed and get under the covers to protect ourselves from the belt. Dad didn't swing the belt very hard. Still, as soon as he'd swing it, all three of us would pretend we were crying under the covers. We knew Dad would stop swinging the moment he thought we were crying. And he always did. When Dad left the room, the three of us would laugh quietly, knowing we'd fooled Dad once again into thinking he was hurting us.

Where was I? Oh, yeah ... so when Mom told me, Joe, and Larry that we couldn't go back to Tip O'Leary's without her or Dad, we promised her we wouldn't. It was an easy promise to make. After almost getting robbed there that day, going back to that area was the last thing I wanted to do. As soon as we finished peeling the labels off our new John Smith sneaks, the three of us headed over to Myers playground, stopping along the way to tie our old sneaks together and toss them up over the telephone wire to join the four pairs of old sneaks already hanging over the wire.

When we got to the playground, we told our friends all about how we almost got robbed. After we told our story, a few guys told stories they'd heard about trouble in the 54th Street area. Then our friend Timmy told the story of how he got his brand-new Converse All Stars stolen right off his feet up near 58th and Willows Avenue, about a half-mile away from Myers playground. Three black teenagers surrounded Timmy, who was 11, and told him to give them his sneaks or they were going to kick his ass. Timmy took off his Converse All Stars, handed them over, and walked home in his socks. I remember thinking how lucky we were that we didn't live near 54th Street or near Willows Avenue. Even though there was trouble brewing all around us, we were still as safe as can be here in our pocket of the neighborhood. Unfortunately, that would change soon, way too soon.

CHAPTER 3
July, 1969:
Unwelcome Visitors

I KNEW DWIGHT was going to cut to the basket as soon as our eyes connected. I'd played so much basketball with Dwight that summer, it had gotten to the point where we knew what each other was going to do without saying a word. Sure enough, Dwight cut to the basket, my bounce-pass met him in stride, he made the lay-up, and we won the game.

It was the first time me and Dwight had ever beaten my older brother, Joe, and Dwight's older brother, Lonny, in a game of two-on-two. And we played them a lot. Dwight and Lonny were the only black kids who played basketball with us at Myers playground. Both of them were really good basketball players. About a year ago, they moved into a house right across the street from the playground. They were two of the nicest kids I'd ever met, white or black. We became friends from the get-go.

"Great game, Dwight," I said as we shook hands on our short walk to the water fountain.

"Yeah, great game, Kev," Dwight replied.

I kept talking just loud enough so that both of our brothers could hear me. "We showed those old guys who the real players are around here."

Both of our older brothers shot us a quick glare as me and Dwight broke up laughing. After we took turns drinking from the water fountain, Dwight and Lonny headed home. They never hung out with us. They'd just come over to Myers playground to play basketball just about every day, and then they'd go home.

Myers playground used to be an orphanage until the early sixties, when it was converted into a playground. The orphanage had three large buildings, each in a different corner of the property. The building closest to the corner of 58th and Kingsessing Avenue had been converted into an indoor gym. The other two buildings were empty and slowly falling apart. Next to the building that was now a gym was a play area with swings, monkey bars, sliding boards, that kind of stuff. Behind the gym, along Kingsessing Avenue, were the basketball courts. The two full courts and four almost-half courts were enclosed by a chain-link fence about three feet high along the near side and eight feet high along the far side, which separated the basketball courts from the tennis courts. The nets on the tennis courts were hardly ever up because hardly anybody ever played tennis there. We used the tennis courts to play other games like box-ball and sock-it-out, two baseball games we played with rubber air balls. We also used the tennis courts to play street hockey. Street hockey was becoming big in the area ever since the Flyers hockey team came to Philly in 1967. The tennis courts were a perfect fit for street hockey games.

Right next to the tennis courts were the metal bleachers along the third base line of one of the two baseball fields that took up more than half of the playground's property. The two baseball fields faced each other and overlapped briefly in the outfield. In the fall, a big part of the baseball outfield became part of the playground's football field.

After our basketball game with Dwight and Lonny, me and Joe got into a game of pinochle. We were playing with two of our friends, sitting on the bleachers along the first base line of the baseball field, not far from the basketball courts. We played a lot of card games in the playground. Pinochle was my favorite. A lot of guys liked to play a card game called "knuckles." In knuckles, the losers get their knuckles whacked over and over with the edge of a full deck of cards. I'd gotten my knuckles whacked a lot. We all did. It hurt like hell. I'd seen some guys get their knuckles hit so hard they'd start bleeding. I liked pinochle a lot more than knuckles, and not just because it was less painful. In pinochle, we played with partners, so the game involved teamwork and a lot of focus.

I learned to play pinochle by watching the older guys play. They played a lot, especially on rainy days. Sometimes, as I watched the older guys play, one of them would have to leave before the game was over. And sometimes, if no other older guys were around, they'd ask me to take his place. I'd feel excited and nervous at the same time. I was getting good at pinochle, but I still had a lot to learn. I didn't want to throw the wrong card and let my teammate down. Over the years, I'd seen how intense these games could get.

It was the same way with basketball. Sometimes, as I watched the older guys play, one of them would twist an ankle and have to sit out. And sometimes, if no other older guys were around, they'd ask me to take his place. Just like with pinochle, I was excited to be playing with the older guys. But I was also nervous. I didn't want to let my teammates down. I probably passed the ball a lot more than I should have. But I knew, if I wanted the older guys to pick me to play again, it was always smarter to pass too much than to shoot too much. The older guys didn't like playing with young guys who came into a game and started launching up shots.

After about a half-hour into our pinochle game, I heard a strange voice yelling, "Foul. That's a foul."

Another voice yelled right back, "No way, man. I got all ball."

The voices were coming from behind me, in the basketball courts. When I turned around from my seat on the bleachers, I saw six black kids I'd never seen before playing a game of three-on-three. They looked to be about three or four years older than me. I was 10. I guess they were around 13 or 14. It was the first time I'd ever seen a group of black kids that age playing basketball at Myers playground.

The only group of black people of *any* age who played basketball at the playground was a group of older guys who were in their twenties and thirties. Every Sunday morning, when the weather was nice enough to play, they'd pull up in three or four cars and park along the Kingsessing Avenue side of the playground. There were usually about 10 to 15 of them. Those older black guys were some of the best basketball players I'd ever seen. Lots of Sunday mornings, after going to early Mass at MBS Church, Dad would take us over to the playground to watch those older black guys play. Dad knew who some of them were. He told us some of them played in a semi-pro basketball league called the Eastern League. I remember thinking how cool it was that I could watch such good players right here in Myers playground.

Anyway, this group of six young black kids that I'd never seen before played basketball for about an hour. Then they left the playground and headed toward 58th Street, where they turned right toward Greenway

Avenue. That part of 58th Street, the block between Greenway Avenue and Woodland Avenue, has had a lot of black families living there for as long as I can remember, even when the rest of the neighborhood was all white. I knew a lot of the black people who lived on that block because that block was part of the newspaper route where me and Joe delivered the *Evening Bulletin* every day. But I didn't remember ever seeing any of those six black kids down there. They must have just moved in.

The next day, the same six black kids came back to Myers playground. They played basketball for about an hour, and then they left. After they left, I could tell some of the older white guys were getting pissed off that these black kids were playing basketball in Myers playground.

"Why the fuck they have to come here?" I overheard one of the older guys say.

Then another one said, "This is our playground. They got their own fucking playground down on 49th Street."

He was talking about the playground on 49th and Kingsessing Avenue. I was never in that playground. But every time I'd ride by it on the "13" trolley, most of the people hanging out there were black. So I guess he was right, there was a playground for blacks at 49th Street. Still, it would be a long walk from 58th Street all the way to 49th Street just to play some basketball, especially when there were some empty courts during the day right here at Myers playground.

The following day, the same six black kids came back to Myers playground again. Us younger guys were in the tennis courts playing box-ball. In box-ball, the pitcher bounced an air ball to the batter who used his fist to hit the ball into play. If we didn't have enough players for outfielders, the ball had to be hit in the infield, or it was an automatic out. Box-ball was the opposite of sock-it-out. We played sock-it-out when we only had a handful of guys. In sock-it-out, there was no pitcher, no infielders, only a couple of outfielders on each team. The hitter would toss the ball up in the air and try to hit it with his fist on its way down. The ball had to be hit on a fly into the outfield. If the ball bounced anywhere in the infield, it was an automatic out.

Between innings in our box-ball game, I looked around and noticed some of the older white guys were digging through the trashcan near the basketball courts, pulling out empty soda bottles. I was pretty sure they weren't digging for bottles to get a two-cents-a-bottle refund, like a lot of us younger kids did. But I had no idea why they were digging for bottles. Minutes later, I found out.

All of a sudden, I heard four or five bursts of glass shattering behind me in the basketball courts. I quickly turned around and saw about 10 older white kids chasing after the six black kids. At first, the black kids looked stunned. Then they took off running, jumped over the short fence, and continued out onto Kingsessing Avenue toward 58th Street. They even left their basketball behind.

After the black kids were out of sight, one of the older guys yelled, "This is our playground. We don't want no fucking niggers around here."

I honestly didn't know the word "nigger" was an insult until I was about seven or eight years old. The word was used so much by so many people in our neighborhood, I just thought it was another way of saying "black person." When I found out the word was an insult, I tried not to use it anymore. I still said it once in a while, usually trying to impress the older guys. But then I'd feel bad that I said it. I figured if I'm mad at somebody because he's an asshole, I should call him an asshole. If he's a punk, I should call him a punk. But by calling someone a "nigger," or a "dago," or a "polock," I'd be insulting a whole nationality of people. And that's not what I had in mind.

I didn't like seeing those black kids getting chased away like that. Just three weeks earlier, at Tip O'Leary's, it was me and my brothers who were outnumbered and being chased. I didn't like that feeling. And I didn't like seeing anybody, black or white, have to feel the same way. I really didn't care that those kids were playing basketball at Myers playground. They weren't bothering anybody. So what was the big deal? Evidently, it was a big deal to some of those older white guys. I guess the only reason they didn't chase Dwight and Lonny out of the playground was because they were playing basketball with us.

I was glad none of the black kids got hurt. But I had a feeling they wouldn't be coming back. And they didn't come back the next day, or the next, or the next. Little did I know that, when they would return, they'd return with a vengeance.

CHAPTER 4
August, 1969:
Retaliation

EVERY DAY OF every summer, all kinds of activities were going on at Myers playground. Most younger kids in our neighborhood signed up for the playground's summer camp. All day, I'd see them walking around in small groups and hear them playing games and singing songs like "Ring Around the Rosie" and "This Old Man." From time to time, I'd hear some of the teenaged camp counselors yelling, "Stay with your group," at the young kids who were wandering off.

Kids our age were on the basketball courts, tennis courts, and baseball fields all day, every day. The rhythm of bouncing basketballs constantly filled the air, along with the loud cracks of wooden baseball bats smashing hard balls into the air.

Most of our summer days at the playground were full of fun and games, except those days our "oldhead" had other ideas. Our "oldhead" is what we called the group of guys who were two and three years older than us who also hung out at Myers playground. They called us their "younghead." But they felt we had to earn the privilege to be called their younghead. So about one or twice a month, they'd put us through their version of boot camp.

I knew how the oldhead-younghead relationship worked. For years, I'd seen *our* oldhead get put to the test by *their* oldhead. Some of their oldhead had just turned 16 and were now driving cars. So their latest antic was to grab a couple of their younghead, throw them in a car, drive them to the

Philly airport, and drop them off there, forcing them to walk about three hours from the airport back to Myers playground.

Most of our oldhead were 14 years old at the time, so they didn't have cars. But they still did some crazy stuff to us. Because so many kids in the neighborhood had newspaper routes, many kids used grocery-shopping carts to deliver the papers. So it wasn't unusual to see a shopping cart or two somewhere in the playground. A lot of times those shopping carts played a part in our oldhead's boot camps.

They would put us younger guys, one at a time, into a shopping cart, which they would push down a concrete ramp into the metal doors that led to a room under Myers gym where all the little league baseball equipment was stored. We all hoped we were put into a shopping cart that had steady front wheels. At least that way we knew we'd go straight down the ramp and smash into the metal doors. Smashing into those doors hurt a lot. But it didn't hurt nearly as much as the times we were pushed down the ramp in a shopping cart with a wobbly front wheel. Those carts would tip over about halfway down the ramp and send us head over heals into the concrete. That really hurt.

Other times, our oldhead would get in two lines, about four feet apart. Then they'd make us run between the two lines as they swung their belts at us. Most of our oldhead hit us with the strap end of their belts. But a few of the guys liked to hit us with their belt buckles. Those guys seemed to get way too much pleasure out of beating up us younger guys. One day, they told our friend Hughie to hug a small tree. When he hugged the tree, they tied his hands together with his belt and left him there for about an hour. Then they decided to hang our friend Sammy from another tree. They lifted Sammy off the ground until he was high enough to put the hood of his coat over a tree limb. Luckily, Sammy wasn't in pain. Because of the angle of the tree limb he was hanging from, most of the pressure was under Sammy's arms, not around his neck. Sammy just hung there looking around with a helpless expression on his face. After a few minutes, two of our saner oldhead finally helped Sammy down.

Even though our oldhead could be tough on us, we knew these boot camps were something we had to go through to earn their respect. We'd seen their oldhead do it to them, and now it was their turn to do it to us. But we also knew there was a big benefit in all of this. We knew that any time we got into fights with older guys from other neighborhoods, our oldhead would be right there by our side, ready to protect their younghead.

Other than an occasional boot-camp day, most summer days at Myers playground were packed with fun from start to finish. At night, the playground was definitely the place to be, not just for kids, but for adults, too. Lots of adults would walk over to the playground to watch the games in the summer basketball and baseball leagues. At the time, Myers had the best leagues in all of Southwest Philly. Night after night, large crowds would gather to watch the games.

Myers summer basketball leagues included the High School League and the Senior League. The High School League games were played earlier than the Senior League games. A lot of the best high school players in our area played in the league. There were usually two games going on, side-by-side, at the same time. That summer, everybody was talking about this tall, skinny black kid from Bartram High School, the public high school in our neighborhood. The kid's name was Joe Bryant. He could jump higher than any high school player I'd ever seen. I liked to watch him dunk the ball in pre-game warm-ups. I often wished he was allowed to dunk in the games. I would have loved to see Joe Bryant flying through the air, slamming the ball through the rim. But they recently outlawed dunking in high school and college basketball. I read in the *Bulletin* that they changed the rule because of a seven-foot-four kid named Lew Alcindor. He was playing at UCLA. Because he was seven-foot-four, the NCAA decided it would be way too easy for him to simply dunk the ball every time he got it. So they changed the rule, and no one in college or high school was allowed to dunk anymore during games. Now the only time I could watch guys dunk was in warm-ups.

After the high school games were over, the Senior League games started. The Senior League was the main attraction, the games everybody wanted to see. The league included some of the best players in the Philly area, including a lot of guys who used to play college basketball or were still playing in college.

The two guys I rooted for the most were Tom Duff and Richie Berberian. Tom Duff played high school basketball at St. Joe's Prep and college basketball at St. Joe's College. I knew Tom because he lived right up the street from us on the corner of Cecil Street and Kingsessing Avenue. Tom was always friendly to me and my brothers. He was tall, played forward, and was a workhorse around the basket. Richie Berberian was a star at West Catholic High School who was now playing basketball at Hiram Scott, a small college in Nebraska. I knew Richie because he worked at Myers playground during the summer. Richie was a great guard with strong legs that sprung him high into the air, so high he could easily shoot over players much taller than him. Not only was Richie a great player, he was also a great guy. Sometimes, when Richie was working at the playground, he would come over to the basketball courts and shoot them up with us. I couldn't believe I was actually shooting baskets with one of the best players in our neighborhood. Most of the real good athletes Richie's age wouldn't even say hello to kids our age, let alone shoot baskets with us.

During the Senior League playoff games, hundreds of people lined the main basketball court two and three rows deep to watch the games. They even set up a loudspeaker system to announce the action to the crowd. Sometimes I couldn't even see the games through the crowd. Whenever I couldn't see, I'd climb to the top of the eight-foot fence that separated the basketball courts from the tennis courts so I could see the action above the crowd.

The crowd often included some of Philly's biggest basketball names. Jack Ramsey was at some of the games. He was the coach of the 76ers at the time. My dad knew Jack Ramsey because he used to coach at St. Joe's when Uncle Jim played there. Jack McKinney was also at some of the games. He was the current coach at St. Joe's. My dad also knew Jack McKinney because he lived right next door to my Uncle John in Drexel Hill, in the suburbs. Whenever I was with my dad watching the games and Jack Ramsey or Jack McKinney was in the crowd, I'd get to shake their hands. I felt like I was shaking hands with basketball royalty. And there was a lot more basketball royalty at some of those games. I saw 76ers guard Hal Greer there. I saw 76ers forward Luke Jackson there. Luke Jackson was six-foot-nine and had a huge upper body. No wonder he got so many rebounds. But as big as Luke Jackson was, his size was nothing compared to Wilt Chamberlain. I'll never forget the night I saw Wilt at the playground. He was seven-foot-one. I couldn't believe any human being could be that big. Wilt wasn't playing for the 76ers at the time. He'd recently been traded to the Los Angeles Lakers just a year after he led the 76ers to the NBA Championship. Wilt was at Myers playground because he grew up just a few miles from the playground, in West Philly across the street from Cobbs Creek Park.

It was amazing to me that I got to see all these great basketball coaches and players at the playground that was right around the corner from our house. I couldn't believe how lucky I was to be a kid growing up in this neighborhood.

Myers playground also had a great baseball league. It was called Little Americans. Every weeknight during the season, an early game and a late game were played on both of the playground's two baseball fields. After each game, every kid on every team, win or lose, got a free water ice from the refreshments room that was tucked into the side of Myers gym. Seemed like every kid in our neighborhood played in Little Americans. Even kids from other neighborhoods that had their own leagues played in Little Americans, including some black kids from other neighborhoods. I always had one or two black kids on my baseball team.

I was used to being around black people. In fact, my first teacher in school was a black lady named Mrs. Hollins. She was my kindergarten teacher at Mitchell School, the public elementary school that was diagonally across the street from MBS. The year I was to start kindergarten was the first year MBS decided it didn't have enough room to have kindergarten classes anymore. So I had to go to kindergarten at Mitchell School. Mrs. Hollins looked like she was in her late forties, tall and thin, with a certain dignity about her in both the way she looked and the way she carried herself. She made me feel safe and comfortable, which I guess is the main job of a kindergarten teacher with a class full of five- and six-year-olds away from their moms for the very first time.

What I remember most about Mrs. Hollins was something that happened one November afternoon. The school's cleaning lady, a white lady, came into our room with tears rolling down her face. She whispered something into Mrs. Hollins' ear. Whatever the cleaning lady said, I got the sense that Mrs. Hollins wanted to break down and cry, too. But she kept biting her upper lip so that she wouldn't cry. I guess she figured that, if she cried, she would upset all us young kids in her classroom. Her inner strength that day really impressed me. Still, seeing her like that, I knew something had to be wrong. I told Mom what happened when she came to get me and walk me home after school. Mom's eyes were red, too. She looked like she'd been crying herself. Mom said the reason everybody was so upset was because, while I was in school, President Kennedy had been shot and killed. At the time, I didn't understand how big a deal that was. But I do know that, when we got home, all the TV shows were cancelled, and every person on every TV station was talking about President Kennedy's death.

Even in my early years at MBS, I always had one or two black kids in my classroom. In fifth grade, a black friend from MBS, named Reggie, came over to our house a few times. He was the first black kid that was ever in our house. Reggie lived near 53rd Street. He was on our fifth- and sixth-grade football team. Because we practiced at Myers playground every weeknight, Reggie would sometimes stop by my house on his way to practice, and we'd walk over to practice together. A few times when Reggie came over, I noticed some of our neighbors peeking out their windows to see who this strange black kid was. But I didn't care. Reggie was a good kid.

I always got along with the black people I knew. So having a black kid or two on my Little Americans baseball team was no big deal to me. What was a big deal was what happened during one of our baseball games on a warm, July night. It was unlike anything I'd ever seen before.

Our team was playing the late game on the baseball field closest to 59th and Chester Avenue, farthest away from the basketball courts. I forget what inning it was, probably the sixth or seventh because the sky was starting to get dark. Our team was up to bat. I wasn't scheduled to bat that inning, so I was sitting on the team bench. Suddenly, I heard loud screams coming from the other baseball field, the one closest to the basketball courts. I looked up and saw about 20 black people, both teenagers and adults, swinging belts and broom handles and throwing bottles and rocks at the mostly white people who had been watching the game from the metal bleachers, but were now running for cover.

Our game came to an immediate stop. Coaches and parents from our field grabbed the little-league baseball bats that were lined up against the chain-link fence in the on-deck areas. Then they all ran up to the other field with bats in hand. There they joined other parents in a big fight along the right-field line. I got as close as I could, while staying out of harm's way, to get a better view of what was going on. Grown white men were swinging baseball bats at grown black men who were swinging back with their belts and broom handles. It looked like a few men on both sides got hit.

Baseball field at Myers playground, scene of the big fight between white and black adults. Photo courtesy of Bill Dorsch.

Within minutes, cop cars with sirens blaring raced into Myers playground through both the Kingsessing Avenue and Chester Avenue entrances. The black guys tried to get away, and most of them did. Two were caught and arrested. Later, when things had settled down, I overheard two older white kids talking:

"Some of those younger niggers looked like the kids we chased off the basketball courts last week," one older white kid said.

"Yeah, I think it was them," said the other, "they looked real familiar."

That's when it occurred to me that this whole fight might have been retaliation for what happened the week before, when those six black kids were chased out of the playground. Whatever the reason, it was, by far, the craziest sight my 10-year-old eyes had ever seen. When the fight was over, I had this sinking feeling in my stomach. And it wasn't just because of what I'd just seen. I was upset because of what it might mean for the future. This was much worse than what happened over on 54th Street, when we were almost robbed at Tip O'Leary's. 54th Street was a half-mile away. It was easy to stay out of trouble there by just staying out of that area. This happened here, at 58th Street, in Myers playground. Just like that, I realized that my favorite place in the world might not be so safe anymore.

Before that fight at Myers playground, there were already a lot of "For Sale" signs on most streets in the area. After the fight, it seemed like there were twice as many. I guess a lot of people decided they'd seen enough. They were moving out.

One morning, I was getting ready to go over to the playground when Mom said to me, "Kevin, before you go out to play, stop around Alden Street and say goodbye to the Jordons. They're moving today."

As soon as I walked through the alley to Alden Street, I couldn't miss the huge moving van parked outside the Jordon's house, completely blocking the narrow, one-way street. When I walked to the Jordon's house to say goodbye, both parents had a redness around their eyes. It looked like they'd both been crying. The Jordons were the third family in the Cecil Street area who'd moved out in the past couple of months. All three times, I noticed that the parents seemed to be upset about leaving. And their kids were usually even more upset. About a month earlier, I saw two of the McSorley brothers crying on the day they were moving out. They were about eight and nine years old, and they obviously didn't want to move. No kid in his right mind would want to move out of this neighborhood. Each time I saw a family moving out, I thought to myself, If they're that upset about moving out, then why are they moving in the first place? After all, things still weren't too bad in our section of the neighborhood. I was glad we weren't moving.

My parents never talked about moving, except when we'd get those phone calls from realtors at dinnertime. One time, I asked Mom why they call all the time.

Mom told me, "They keep tellin' me we should sell our house now, before too many blacks move in."

"Why do they say that?" I asked her.

"They say once the blacks move in, all the houses will be worth a lot less money."

"Is it true?" I asked.

"I don't know what to believe," Mom said. "I just want them to stop callin' me."

A few days later, I heard more about all this real estate stuff. I was shopping for my mom over at the grocery store on the corner of 58th and Chester Avenue, across the street from Myers playground. As I was waiting in line to check out, I overheard Mr. Jenkins talking to another man. Mr. Jenkins liked to hang out near the check-out counter, talking to other neighbors who came into the store to buy groceries. Both Mr. Jenkins and the man he was talking to looked like they were in their forties.

"Now's the time to get the hell out of this neighborhood," I heard Mr. Jenkins say. "They're already livin' on 54th Street and I hear they're movin' in on 55th Street, too."

The other man chimed in, "They'll be up here at 58th Street before you know it."

"My realtor told me," said Mr. Jenkins, "if I wait 'til then, I won't get nearly as much money for my house as I can get right now. I know I ain't waitin'. I'm movin' the hell out of here before all the niggers move in."

My parents didn't want to move. Besides, if they did move, they'd probably have to pay more for a new house than they were paying for our house now. And they were already having a hard enough time making ends meet. I could see the frustration on Mom's face whenever she'd sit down at the dining room table with all the bills spread out in front of her. She'd often say paying bills was like "robbing Peter to pay Paul." I had a feeling at least one bill didn't get paid each month. I think Mom's strategy was to make sure it was a different bill each month. Every so often, I'd answer the phone, and it would be someone we owed money to, asking to talk to my parents. Whenever that happened, Mom always told us to say, "I'm sorry. My parents aren't home right now." So that's what I'd say.

I figured if my parents didn't have enough money to pay all the bills now, there's no way they had enough money to pay even more for a new house. And that was fine with me. I didn't want to move. Even though we almost got robbed at Tip O'Leary's, even though there'd been some trouble at Myers playground, I was still having way too much fun in our neighborhood to even think about living anywhere else.

CHAPTER 5
September, 1969:
Tradition Turns to Terror

IT WAS A hot, September, Sunday afternoon, the day of West Catholic High School's first home football game of the season. West Catholic played its home games at Bartram High School's Field at 58th and Elmwood Avenue. The field was about a half-mile walk from our house. That half-mile walk, that day, turned out to be more action-packed than the game itself.

For as long as I can remember, every time West Catholic played at home, hundreds of people, mostly white, would walk the traditional route down 58th Street to get to the game. The games were usually on Sunday afternoons at one o'clock. When we'd walk to the games, we'd pass that block of homes on 58th Street where black people have lived for years, the block between Greenway Avenue and Woodland Avenue that was part of me and Joe's newspaper route. In past years, we'd walk back and forth to West Catholic football games without a care in the world, often stopping along the way at a store at 58th and Woodland Avenue that had the best milkshakes in the neighborhood. But this year, walking down that block of 58th Street felt different. A lot more black people had recently moved into that part of the neighborhood, including a lot of the black guys who were in the big fight at Myers playground. Ever since that fight, I had a feeling the walks to the West Catholic football games might not be so carefree anymore. Because me and Joe delivered newspapers down there, we knew that a lot of the older black guys were now hanging out at 58th and Greenway Avenue.

We knew some of them. In fact, we were in a lot of their homes every week when we had to collect money from our newspaper customers. Evidently, at least one of the older black guys knew who we were, too.

One afternoon, when me and Joe were delivering newspapers down there, five black kids about our age started walking across Greenway Avenue directly toward us. It looked like they were going to mess with us. I turned to Joe and whispered, "Get ready, here they come." I had no idea what we were going to do, I just wanted to make sure Joe knew they were coming.

Just then, one of the older black guys hanging out on Greenway Avenue yelled over to the younger black kids. "Hey. They cool," he said, "they're my paperboys."

The younger kids stopped in their tracks, turned around, and walked back across the street. I immediately glanced over to see which of the older black guys had looked out for us. It was Ronnie. Ronnie was about 15 years old. We delivered the *Bulletin* to Ronnie's house. Whenever I went to his house to collect, Ronnie's mother usually answered the door. She was a nice lady who always gave me a 10-cent tip. Sometimes when I was in their house, Ronnie would be there. He never said "hi," but he always gave me a nod. I was surprised Ronnie protected me and Joe the way he did. But I was sure glad he did.

Anyway, on this hot, September afternoon, just a few weeks before my 11th birthday, there must have been about 10 of us, including me and my brothers Joe and Larry, walking down 58th Street to the West Catholic football game. Mom had given me and my brothers just enough money to buy a ticket for the game. But we had no intention of buying a ticket. We were going to use the money to buy a milkshake on the way home.

Our plan was to climb the 10-foot, chain-link fence behind the bleachers on the West Catholic side of the field. We'd wait until West Catholic made a big play. That usually got the attention of the adults from West Catholic who were trying to make sure kids like us didn't sneak into the game. Once we'd hear the roar of the West Catholic fans, we'd quickly scale the fence and try to blend in with the people who were already in the stands.

As we began our half-mile walk down 58th Street to the game, I wondered how the black teenagers who were new to the neighborhood would feel about having all these white people walking through what was now their turf. I figured if there was going to be any trouble, it would happen near Greenway Avenue. And that's where it happened. As soon as we got halfway between Greenway Avenue and Woodland Avenue, about

10 black teenagers came running up behind us from Greenway Avenue, throwing bottles and rocks. It looked like they were aiming for a group of our oldhead who were walking right behind us.

Us younger kids took off running down 58th Street toward the football field. We were running as fast as we could, along with some older adults and young couples with little kids who were also on their way to the football game. Our oldhead stayed to fight. The fighting drifted into the middle of 58th Street. Traffic came to a stop in both directions. Some of the white guys snapped car antennas off parked cars and began swinging them at the black guys who were swinging back with broom handles and belts. It looked like a few guys, white and black, got hit and were bleeding. Within a couple minutes, two cop cars that had been parked just a couple blocks away, outside the football field, raced up 58th Street to break up the fight. The cops, nightsticks in hand, sprung from their cars out onto the street. Everybody who was fighting scattered. The black guys ran back toward Greenway Avenue. The white guys ran down 58th Street to try to blend in with the crowd waiting in line to get into the football game.

Outside the football field, I could see the shock on the faces of some of the older adults and little kids who had been walking near us when the fight started. A couple kids about five or six years old were still crying as their parents tried to calm them down.

A few Sundays later, the day of West Catholic's second home football game, a lot less people walked the traditional route down 58th Street to get to the game. Many people walked an extra half-mile out of their way to avoid the area where the fight broke out. I was perfectly willing to walk the extra half-mile myself.

I remember me and my friends met at Myers playground to walk to the game together. Our oldhead was meeting there, too. I overheard one of our oldhead say:

"Fuck them. I've walked down 58th Street to West Catholic games my whole life. And I'm walkin' down 58th Street today. Who's comin' with me?"

The rest of our oldhead definitely looked like they were getting ready to join him. Many were loading the pockets of their pants with rocks and the pockets of their coats with bottles. My friends, including my brothers Joe and Larry, decided to walk down 58th Street as well. I went along with them. I really didn't want to. But there was no way I was going to admit I was afraid.

As usual, we all walked on the side of 58th Street that had no houses. On that side of 58th Street was a four-foot stone wall that surrounded a big nursing home. When we got to Greenway Avenue, everything looked quiet. But once we passed the end of the nursing home's wall, close to Woodland Avenue, bottles and rocks came flying at us from a car-repair lot that was on the same side of the street where we were walking. The black teenagers had been hiding in the car-repair lot, waiting for the right moment to attack.

Just like last time, us younger guys ran up ahead, while the older guys stayed and fought. As I looked back, I could see that the fighting had moved into the middle of 58th Street, stopping traffic in both directions. Then things got even crazier.

As more and more black kids from the area joined the fight, the battle quickly drifted across Woodland Avenue and kept getting closer and closer to the railroad tracks that crossed 58th Street between Woodland Avenue and Elmwood Avenue. Long freight trains crossed those railroad tracks three or four times a day. Those trains were so long they'd stop traffic for 15 to 20 minutes at a time. As I was watching the fight, I suddenly heard loud bells ringing behind me. When I glanced back, I saw the red lights flashing on the long, white, train-crossing gates as they slowly descended into their positions across 58th Street, blocking traffic in both directions to make way for the oncoming train.

Us younger guys quickly made our way across the railroad tracks. But the older guys were still fighting. They had no idea a train was coming. If they didn't cross the tracks before the train got there, they'd be trapped on the other side for at least 15 minutes, having to fight the black kids who, by this time, outnumbered them by about two to one.

We all started yelling at the top of our lungs. I yelled, "Yo guys, the train's coming! Look behind you, the train's coming!"

Good thing one of the older guys heard us. When he glanced back and saw the train-crossing gates were down and flashing, he yelled over to the other guys who looked back and saw that a train was coming. Then, as if on cue, they all stopped fighting, turned, and sprinted toward the railroad tracks. They literally made their way across the tracks just seconds before a huge locomotive crossed 58th Street.

I couldn't believe what I'd just seen. It was just one more thing I'd seen in the past three months that had blown my mind: the black kids trying to steal our new sneaks, the white kids attacking the black kids who were playing basketball, the big fight at Myers playground, and now this.

Each time, I couldn't believe what I was seeing was really happening. The action and tension were unlike anything I'd ever seen except on TV or in a movie. The first thought that would flash through my mind was, Did I just see what I think I saw? And each time, the answer was yes. And each time, it was really scary.

CHAPTER 6
January, 1970:
The Winter Everything Changed

LOTS OF FIGHTS were breaking out between black kids and white kids throughout the neighborhood. Some fights I saw. Others I heard about. In one fight, a few months earlier, near 55th and Chester Avenue, a 16-year-old white kid got stabbed in the head with a screwdriver. Doctors had to insert a metal plate in the kid's head to save his life.

Nearly all the fights I heard about or saw involved guys older than me. I was just 11. Me and my friends were still too young to be part of the action. But I could feel the racial tension every time I saw a group of white kids pass a group of black kids on the sidewalk. There was always the shoulder-to-shoulder bumping, with neither side willing to give up any ground. Most times the shoulder bumps were the end of it, especially if adults or cops were nearby. Other times, the shoulder bumps were just the beginning.

One afternoon, I saw shoulder-to-shoulder bumps explode into a brief but violent fight. I had just turned the corner from Cecil Street onto Chester Avenue on my way to the Vittle Vat, my favorite sandwich shop. The Vittle Vat was just a few stores down on the right. Up ahead, I saw five of our oldhead walking along Chester Avenue toward 57th Street. Ahead of them, I saw five black kids, 14 or 15 years old, about the same age as our oldhead, walking in the opposite direction toward 58th Street. The two groups were headed right for each other. At the pace they were walking, it looked like they would pass each other right in front of Cahill's Tavern, on the corner of Alden Street and Chester Avenue. I had a feeling there might be trouble. So instead of walking into the Vittle Vat, I waited outside the store's front door to watch the groups pass each other. I knew if things got out of hand, I could easily run into the Vittle Vat where I'd be safe.

As I expected, all five white kids banged shoulders with all five black kids. Then, instead of both groups continuing on, one of the white kids turned around and pushed one of the black kids in the back. The black kid swung around and, in the same motion, threw a punch that hit the white kid square in the middle of his face. Blood gushed from his nose, and the fight was on with all 10 kids throwing punch after punch after punch. The action was furious. As fast as the fight started, it ended just as quickly when three older white guys who were in Cahill's ran out to see what was going on. The black kids, thinking the white guys from Cahill's were going to jump in on the fight, took off running.

As winter set in, the cold weather didn't bother me as much as it usually did. I hated the cold. But that winter, as the weather got colder, I noticed that the streets got safer, with fewer kids hanging out on the corners. For the first winter in my life, I didn't mind the cold at all. Plus, when the weather got colder, I got to hang out at my second favorite place in the world: the indoor gym at Myers playground.

Myers gym was in a two-story, stone building, one of three stone buildings that were part of the old orphanage. The gym was in the building closest to 58th and Kingsessing Avenue. Myers gym had one full court for basketball that was much smaller than the full courts outside; the free throw line was way too close to half court. The basketball court's far sideline butted up against one of the gym's exterior walls. Along that wall was a wooden radiator cover, about five feet high, which extended from one end of the court to the other. Above the radiator cover was a wall of small rectangular windows that rose all the way up to the gym's ceiling.

That radiator cover served as our front row seats to watch the best basketball players in the gym go at it. Because the gym only had one basketball court, it was impossible for an 11-year-old like me to get into a game. So we'd pull ourselves up onto the top of the radiator cover and sit there, with our backs against the windows, to watch the older guys play.

A lot of those guys were really good players. I liked to study the moves of my two favorite players, Jim McCurry and Bobby Brewers. Neither of those guys played on their high school basketball team. I don't think they even wanted to play for their high school team. They just loved playing pick-up basketball every day after school. I always thought both of those guys were every bit as good as, or even better than, some of the neighborhood guys who played on their high school basketball teams.

Next to the basketball court was an open space the same size as the basketball court. Next to the open space, just past a narrow walkway, was another large room with a small stage that was used for neighborhood talent shows, concerts, plays, stuff like that.

Myers gym was packed every day after school. Because the gym was always crowded, we weren't allowed to bring balls into the gym. So we had to get creative to come up with games to play in the open area next to the basketball court. Lots of days, we'd play football using somebody's wool hat wrapped up in black, electrical tape. Then we'd play kick-hockey using that same roll of electrical tape as our hockey puck.

Other times, when the gym got too crowded, we'd go out in the cold and play football. We'd play full-contact, tackle football with no pads. Our games were usually four-against-four or five-against-five. We played on a small section of grass that was about 30 yards long by 20 yards wide. We knocked each other around pretty good. We all got our share of bumps and bruises, but no serious injuries. Seemed like most serious football injuries happened when we were playing with helmets and pads during MBS football season.

Those tackle football games in the playground were a lot of fun. I always found playing sports to be a lot more fun when there were no coaches and parents around, just a bunch of us kids picking sides, playing the games, and working out our disagreements. Our outdoor football games got even more hard-hitting in December and January once the NFL playoffs got under way. We'd name our teams after the teams that were still alive in the NFL playoffs, and pretend we were some of the best players on those teams. Unfortunately, none of us could ever call our team the Eagles. The Eagles were awful. Every year they were one of the worst teams in the NFL. The last time they made the playoffs was the year they won the championship, back in 1960. I was just two years old back then, so I had no memory of that Eagles team. As far back as my memory went, the Eagles had never been in a playoff game my entire life. So we'd name our teams after teams like the Raiders, the Chiefs, the Cowboys, and the Vikings, teams that were in the playoffs year after year.

That winter, when we were playing football outside, I could see that more and more black kids were playing basketball on the outside courts, even on cold days. None of the black kids ever came into Myers gym. It just didn't happen. But they definitely knew we were in there.

One day after school, I was sitting up on the gym's radiator cover, my back resting against the wall of windows, watching the older guys play basketball. All of a sudden, I heard "POP … POP … POP … POP!"

The sounds were coming from the windows at the other end of the court. I looked over and saw what seemed like a hundred small pieces of glass raining down onto the court. Four windows had been shattered. The kids who were sitting on the radiator cover closest to the broken windows jumped down onto the court. Four of the players who were near the windows when they shattered ran to the other side of the court, their hands protecting their heads from the falling glass. There, lying in the middle of the court, were five rocks ranging from the size of a golf ball to the size of a baseball. Luckily, the rocks didn't hit anybody. All the guys who were near the falling glass were now standing on the other side of the court, combing through their hair with their fingers, searching for small pieces of glass. It took Jimbo and Ricky a long time to search through their hair. They both had hair down to their shoulders. A lot of the older guys were growing their hair down to their shoulders. I thought the long hair looked cool. But as cool as it looked, it sure made searching for small pieces of glass a lot harder.

Immediately after the windows shattered, one of the playground workers, a guy in his twenties named Sam, ran outside to try to catch whoever threw the rocks. Minutes later, when Sam came back into the gym, one of the older guys asked him, "Didya catch 'em?"

"Nah," Sam replied as he walked over to the court, a dust pan in one hand and a broom in the other, to help pick up the glass, "they were already down near Greenway Avenue."

"Any idea who it was?"

"Didn't see anybody's face, but from behind, it looked like four young black kids."

After that day, it wasn't unusual to see two or three of the small windows near the basketball court boarded-up until the playground workers got a chance to replace the glass. And when they finally did replace the glass, it was usually just a matter of time before another bunch of rocks were thrown through another group of windows. By the end of that winter, we came to expect that the windows would get smashed, the same way we came to expect more and more fights that were breaking out all around us. Racial trouble was fast becoming part of day-to-day life. And I was beginning to realize that I'd better get used to it. Our neighborhood was never again going to be anything close to the peaceful area it used to be.

As soon as the weather got a little warmer, we were back on the outside courts, playing basketball. Only now, it wasn't unusual anymore for groups of black kids to come into the playground to play basketball, too. And it wasn't long before the outside basketball courts turned into a battleground. Sometimes when black kids were playing on the courts, white kids would attack with bottles and rocks. Sometimes when we were playing, black kids would attack us. So we were always on the lookout.

It reminded me of something Dad taught me about basketball. Dad always said, "When you're playing defense, keep your head on a swivel. See your man. See the ball. See your man. See the ball."

Now, whenever I was playing on the outside courts at Myers, I'd try to keep my head on an even bigger swivel, thinking, See your man, see the ball, and see if we're about to get attacked.

The first time we got attacked on the outside courts, we were playing a half-court game of three-on-three. When the ball went out of bounds, I took a quick look around for any signs of trouble. Everything looked cool. The instant we started playing again, a bottle smashed just a few feet from where I was standing. Then four or five more bottles smashed all around us. I looked over and saw about a dozen black kids with belts and broom handles, running toward us. They were nowhere in sight just a few seconds before. They were probably hiding on the side porch on the Kingsessing Avenue side of Myers gym, which we couldn't see from the basketball courts.

My brother Joe grabbed the basketball and yelled, "Go to the Old House."

The six of us ran as fast as we could toward the building we called the "Old House." It was one of the old stone buildings from the orphanage, the one that sat in the corner of the playground closest to 59th and Kingsessing Avenue. The building was empty and slowly falling apart. Lying in and around the crumbling building were pieces of stone that had come loose from the outside walls, chunks of plaster that had fallen from the inside walls, and slabs of asphalt tile that we had ripped off the building's roof during our roof-tile fights that we would have among ourselves for fun.

As soon as the six of us got to the Old House, we all grabbed the closest things we could find to throw back at the black kids, who were still running toward us. Once we started throwing stuff back, the black kids came to a stop, stood their ground, and kept throwing stuff back at us. The back-and-forth air battle continued for a good five minutes until two playground workers finally caught wind of what was going on and ran over to break things up.

The outside basketball courts were now a disputed territory. The black kids now thought the courts were theirs. We thought the courts were still ours. Because the courts were now a battleground, we stopped hanging out in that part of the playground. Instead, we started hanging out near the Old House. We still played a lot of basketball, although many times we'd have to clear broken glass off the court before we could play. The difference was, as soon as we were done playing basketball, we'd go back to the Old House to hang out. Hanging out there gave us more time to get ready if a fight was coming and a lot more ammunition to use in those fights.

Most of our fights at that time were like the fight I just described: long-range air battles. Both groups would yell racial stuff back and forth from one part of the playground to the other. Then we'd throw stuff back and forth at each other until the cops showed up, or the playground workers came over to break things up. It was during those fights that I first felt like I was no longer just a bystander. On a small scale, at age 11, I was becoming part of the action. We were no longer just a group of kids who got together to have fun and play sports all day. We were becoming a group of kids who had to stick together to defend ourselves, the same way the black kids had to stick together to defend themselves.

Even though our situation at Myers playground was starting to get more dangerous, it was nothing compared to what was going on less than a block away. That's where a lot of the older white teenagers were now hanging out, in front of a corner store called Dirty Annie's.

CHAPTER 7
April, 1970:
The Dirty Annies

STARTED SEEING them there every day after school. About 15 to 20 white guys, around 15 to 17 years old, were now hanging out a half-block from my house, at the corner of Alden Street and Chester Avenue, in front of a small store called Dirty Annie's.

I knew who half the guys were. They were the older guys who were always playing basketball inside Myers gym. Some of the other guys I recognized. They used to hang out at 58th and Willows Avenue. I remember seeing them up there when me and my brother Joe still had our newspaper route.

Up until about a year earlier, every day after school, me and Joe, with our red wagon, would walk about a half-mile up 58th Street to the *Bulletin* branch office, a dungy little room in the side of a building near the corner of 58th and Willows Avenue.

As soon the *Bulletin* truck pulled up and delivered the day's papers, we'd get in line, get our 50 papers, and get going back to our section of the neighborhood. We delivered about half our papers to homes on Kingsessing Avenue, between 56th Street and 57th Street. The other half we delivered on 57th Street, between Kingsessing Avenue and Greenway Avenue.

The only other street we delivered newspapers to was the block of 58th Street between Greenway Avenue and Woodland Avenue, where a lot of black people had lived for years. I could never understand why that block of

58th Street was part of our newspaper route. We had to walk past a whole city block full of houses that weren't on our route just to get there. Seemed like whoever designed these routes could have done a better job. We did a lot of walking every day, but we were making about eight dollars a week. So we both got four dollars a week in spending money, which wasn't bad for kids our age.

Once we left the *Bulletin* branch office with our newspapers, one of us would pull the wagon while the other walked behind to make sure none of the papers fell off, especially those Sunday papers. They were really thick, packed with a lot of advertising inserts. The Saturday newspapers were so thin we didn't even need our wagon. We'd just carry the papers in our canvas bags with the shoulder strap. The *Evening Bulletin* logo was printed on the side of the canvas bag along with the slogan, "Nearly everybody reads the *Bulletin*." The slogan was true. Nearly everybody *did* read the *Bulletin*. It was the most popular newspaper in Philly. And our job was to make sure the *Bulletin* was on our customers' front steps, waiting for them with all the day's news when they got home from work.

A lot of paperboys were using metal shopping carts to deliver papers. Those shopping carts with their deep basket made delivering newspapers so much easier than our wagon. But Mom wouldn't let us use a shopping cart. She said they weren't our property, and she never wanted to see us with one. So we didn't use them, most of the time. Sometimes, if the newspapers were really thick, and me and Joe happened to see an empty shopping cart on the street, we'd borrow it for the day. But we'd never bring one home. Mom would have flipped out on us. When we were done with the shopping cart, we'd just leave it on the street corner where another paperboy was likely to use it to deliver his newspapers.

Across the street from the *Bulletin* branch office, on the corner of 58th and Willows Avenue, was a sandwich shop called The Sunshine Inn. A lot of the older paperboys who lived in that area hung out at The Sunshine Inn. At that time, in 1968 and 1969, a lot more black people were living in the 58th and Willows Avenue area, compared to our part of the neighborhood. So a lot more fighting was going on up there. Some of the first street fights I'd ever seen were between the white kids who hung out at The Sunshine Inn and black kids from the neighborhood. A lot of those fights were right in front of the *Bulletin* office. Me and Joe would watch the fights as we sat in our red wagon, waiting for the *Bulletin* truck to get there. Some of those white guys who hung out at The Sunshine Inn were really tough fighters.

In the years that followed, the number of white guys hanging out at The Sunshine Inn kept shrinking as the number of black kids hanging out in that area kept growing. So now the guys who used to hang out at The Sunshine Inn were hanging out in our section of the neighborhood, the only section that was still mostly white. There, in front of Dirty Annie's store, it was as if all the older white guys in our entire neighborhood had merged into the last remaining white gang their age.

When I say "gang," I don't mean a formal gang like the Pagans and Warlocks motorcycle gangs. There were no initiations, no gang leaders, none of that stuff. In our neighborhood, a gang was just a group of guys who all hung out together. Because all these guys were now hanging out in front of Dirty Annie's store, it wasn't long before the gang itself was called the Dirty Annies.

I saw the Dirty Annies hanging out there every day. So much of my everyday life was centered right there at that intersection. For one thing, I went to Dirty Annie's store a lot. We all did. Dirty Annie's was a messy, disorganized store. I'd often have to step around half-opened cardboard boxes sitting in the middle of the floor just to get to the ice-cream freezer in the back. As messy as the store was, Dirty Annie's sold just about everything an 11-year-old kid like me could want: candy, gum, Tastykakes, ice cream sandwiches, popsicles, soda, comic books. They even sold model cars and airplanes plus the glue to put the models together. That glue brings to mind a whole other story I'll get to a bit later. Dirty Annie's also sold the pink air balls and the white pimple balls that we used for just about every game we played on the streets.

We'd lose a lot of air balls. Many would get hit so high in the air they'd end up on one of the flat roofs of a nearby row home. We also lost a lot of air balls in the sewers. The balls would roll down the street and into the sewer, usually with one of us racing behind to try to stop it.

Whenever an air ball got hit up on a roof, there was no getting it back for a while. Our only hope was that some family on the street would need their roof fixed. Every time we'd see a roofer arrive with that awful-smelling tar pit attached to the back of his truck, we'd walk right up to him. He knew what we were going to ask. We wanted him to throw down any air balls he found on the roofs. All the roofers would do it for us. And the really nice roofers, once they got up on the roof, would take a quick walk up and down all the roofs of the entire row of homes, looking for air balls to throw down to us. Sometimes the roofer would throw down as many as 20 air balls. It was as if air balls were falling from the sky. The scene on the street became a mad scramble as all us kids tried to gather as many air balls as we could. The "finders keepers" rule was in effect.

Whenever air balls went down the sewer, we had another strategy. We would lift the heavy metal sewer cover to see how far down the ball went. Sometimes, after a big rain, the water in the sewer would be backed up, so our air ball would be floating not too far from ground level. If the ball looked gettable, the kid who weighed the least would be lowered, head first, into the sewer so he could try to grab the ball out of the water. Usually the skinniest kid in our group was Charlie. The two biggest guys in our group would each grab hold of one of Charlie's ankles and lower him into the sewer until he was able to grab our ball plus any other balls that were down there. If the water level in the sewer was low, and the ball was too far down, we'd go to Dirty Annie's and buy another ball.

Another reason I was around Dirty Annie's a lot was because my dad bartended right across the street at Cahill's Tavern. Dad usually bartended two nights a week, after working nine to five as a bookkeeper for Penn Central Railroad. I visited Dad at Cahill's just about every night he bartended.

One more reason I was around Dirty Annie's a lot was because the Vittle Vat, my favorite sandwich shop, was also right across the street. Over the years, I ate literally hundreds of sandwiches from the Vittle Vat. Mom was so busy with all of us kids, she'd often tell us to go get cheesesteaks at the Vittle Vat and put it on our bill. Sometimes our bill there got pretty high. Whenever that happened, the nice lady who owned the Vittle Vat would quietly take me or one of my brothers aside and ask us to tell Mom to give her a call.

Because I spent so much time near the Dirty Annies hangout, I saw those guys get into a lot of fights with black kids. I was always impressed at how all the Dirty Annies stuck together, always ready to fight for each other. They had that "all-for-one, one-for-all" attitude that seemed to give them a big advantage every time I saw them fight. And a lot of times, I saw them fight right out the front window of our house.

Our block of Cecil Street was unusual. Most blocks of row homes had houses on both sides of the street. Our block of Cecil Street only had houses on one side of the street. The entire block of land on the other side of Cecil Street belonged to a Presbyterian church. We called the Presbyterian church the "public church." We figured that if kids who don't go to Catholic school go to public school, then adults who don't go to Catholic church must go to public church.

The church building itself was on the corner of 58th and Chester Avenue. It was a big, beautiful stone building with four spires that were so high in the air one of the spires got struck by lightning during a big storm a couple summers earlier. The church minister's house and the Sunday-school building were closer to the Kingsessing Avenue end of the property. In between all the buildings was a large grass field that gave us a clear view across 58th Street and into Myers playground.

Because there were no houses across the street from our house, there was a lot more open space for some wild street fights between the Dirty Annies and the black kids from 58th and Greenway Avenue. I remember the first night I saw them fight outside our house. It was a Saturday night, just after 10 o'clock. *Mannix*, the detective show me and my brothers were watching on TV, had just started.

"What was that?" I yelled, after hearing glass breaking and kids yelling right in front of our house.

We all ran over to our front window to see what was going on. A big street fight was under way. I lowered the window shade all the way down. Then me and my brothers watched all the action, peeking through the sides of the drawn shade. Mom was on the phone, calling the cops.

About 10 black guys from Greenway Avenue were on the left. About 10 Dirty Annies were on the right. When the fight started, both gangs ran at each other as a group, then quickly squared off into a series of one-on-one fights, the way hockey players square off during a fight in a Flyers game. Only this was much more violent. Broom handles and belts were swinging. Punches were flying. It was intense. I watched in amazement at how brutal it was. My 11-year-old mind couldn't process all the action fast enough.

As the fight went on, I spotted Jim McCurry, one of the Dirty Annies who I always liked to watch play basketball in Myers gym. Jim was swinging his belt buckle in the air as he rushed toward the black kid he was matched-up with. When he jerked his belt forward, the buckle landed squarely on the kid's jaw. To avoid getting hit in return, Jim immediately started back-peddling with the same stop-on-a-dime quickness that made him such a good basketball player. I couldn't help but think how ironic it was; I was now learning street-fighting moves from the same guy whose basketball moves I liked to study.

After about a minute or two of intense fighting, I could hear the sirens from the cop cars getting louder and louder as they got closer to our street. Both groups scattered. The black kids ran toward Kingsessing Avenue. The white kids ran toward Chester Avenue. During the fight, I saw a lot of guys get hit, but no one got hit hard enough to fall down.

The following weekend, in another fight in front of our house, someone did get knocked down. In that fight, a black guy got hit in the ribs with a broom handle and went down right in the middle of the street. Because there were more white guys than black guys in the fight that night, the black guy who fell was surrounded by three or four Dirty Annies. He immediately got into a fetal position, the way football players do when they recover a fumble. Only he was using his arms to protect his head, not a football, against the kicks, broom handles, and belt buckles that continued to pummel him until the cops showed up and everyone, except him, took off running. I'd seen people get beat up that bad on TV, but I never saw anybody get beat up that bad in real life. It was animalistic, like a pack of wolves pouncing on a fallen prey. Evidently, the kid wasn't as hurt as I thought he might be. The cops helped him get up off the ground. Then they helped him into the back seat of the cop car and off they went.

Every time I'd watch the Dirty Annies fight in front of our house, I found myself getting a sinking feeling in my stomach. And it wasn't just because of how violent the fights were. I think it was beginning to dawn on me that, in just a few years, I'd be as old as a lot of the Dirty Annies were. And, as dangerous as this neighborhood was getting, someday soon, it might be me out there, like the Dirty Annies, on the front lines battling in the streets.

The Dirty Annies got into lots of fights with black kids that spring, and they won a lot of those fights, which meant more black kids got hurt than Dirty Annies. Word started spreading throughout Southwest Philly about the Dirty Annies, all the fights they were in, and how tough they were. They were becoming the most talked-about gang in Southwest Philly. And it wasn't long before they became one of the most talked-about gangs in *all* of Philly.

CHAPTER 8
June, 1970:
Protest March

AT THE TIME, most black teenagers from Southwest Philly went to John Bartram Public High School. Bartram High was in the middle of a white neighborhood, at 67th and Elmwood Avenue. So a lot of black kids who went to Bartram had to take a bus to get to school.

The Bartram students who lived north of our area took the "G" bus to school each day. The "G" bus traveled from West Philly to South Philly, snaking its way through the streets of Southwest Philly along the way. When the "G" bus traveled through our section of the neighborhood, it went straight through 58th Street. So every day after school, bus after bus packed with mostly black students passed right by the corner of 58th and Chester Avenue, just a half-block from the Dirty Annies hangout. The situation had trouble written all over it. And it almost led to a race riot.

The way I heard it, the trouble, at first, was limited to racial stuff being yelled back and forth between the Bartram students and the Dirty Annies as the buses passed by. There are two sides to the rest of the story.

A newspaper article would later quote some of the Dirty Annies who said the black kids on the buses were throwing stuff out the windows at them as the buses passed by. So they began throwing stuff back at the buses, including rocks and bottles.

The same newspaper article quoted some Bartram students who said they never threw anything at the Dirty Annies. They said the Dirty Annies were throwing stuff at their buses for no reason at all.

One afternoon, I saw one of the "G" buses get attacked on my walk to Myers playground. As I waited for the red light to change so I could cross 58th Street at Chester Avenue, a "G" bus packed with black kids passed by me. A couple of the black kids sitting next to open windows called me a "honky" as the bus passed by. I immediately gave them the finger, and watched as the bus headed up toward Springfield Avenue. All of a sudden, I saw six or seven Dirty Annies jump out from behind parked cars along 58th Street, firing rocks and bottles at the bus, which tried to pick up speed to get out of harm's way.

One day, the Bartram students who rode the "G" bus to school every day decided to stage a protest. It happened one Friday afternoon. I remember sitting in my sixth-grade classroom in MBS, glancing up at the clock, waiting for the weekend to start. Just then, I heard static coming from the loudspeaker, which hung high up on the wall above the blackboard. There were always a few seconds of static every time the loudspeaker was turned on. An announcement was coming. After a few seconds, I heard the soothing voice of Sister Maria Katrina, the young nun who was our new principal. Of the three principals we had in my years at MBS, Sister Maria Katrina was by far the nicest and the prettiest. Sister told us, over the loudspeaker, that we were being let out of school early. She also said we all had to go straight home. She didn't say why.

As we left the school building, I noticed more parents than usual standing around in the schoolyard, waiting to walk the younger kids home. Something weird was going on. I looked around and spotted Mrs. Davis, one of our neighbors who had two young kids at MBS. So I walked over to her to try to find out what was going on.

"Hi, Mrs. Davis. How ya doin'?"

"Oh, hi, Kevin," she replied, "I'm fine."

"Mrs. Davis," I asked, "why are so many parents here?"

Mrs. Davis explained, "I got a phone call and was told that hundreds of Bartram students are walking in a protest march, and they're headed toward our neighborhood. There might be trouble. Make sure you wait for your younger brothers and go right home."

"How close are they?" I asked.

"I'm not sure," Mrs. Davis said, "just get home as soon as you can."

"I will. Thanks, Mrs. Davis."

Mrs. Davis was like so many parents in our neighborhood who looked out for all us kids, not just her own. I felt like I had adults looking out for me on every street in our area, adults I knew I could count on for help in any way, at any time. When Mrs. Davis told me about the Bartram students, I had a feeling it might have something to do with the buses. Sure enough, instead of riding the buses home that day, the Bartram students decided to walk the bus route home to protest all the trouble that was happening on their rides home from school. When the protest march got under way, the cops must have figured that the Bartram students would be passing through our neighborhood at about the same time all the kids from MBS would be getting out of school. So they decided to close MBS early so we could all get home before the protest got to our area. It was always fun to get out of school early, but this was different. I felt a weird kind of excitement like when a big snowstorm is on its way.

As soon as I saw my brothers Joe and Larry in the schoolyard, I told them about the protest march that was headed our way. We waited for our younger brothers, Marty and Steven, who were in third grade and first grade at the time. Then we walked home. When we turned onto Cecil Street, Mom was outside on our front steps waving for us to hurry. She had just gotten back from the grocery store. On her way home from the store, Mom ran into a neighbor who told her about the protest march. So Mom knew what was coming.

"You boys go inside, get a snack, and watch TV," Mom said, "'cause you're not going out 'til this is over."

"Can't we watch from the porch?" asked Larry, knowing we'd have a clear view across the public church grounds onto 58th Street, where the Bartram students were expected to march.

"OK, you can watch from the porch," Mom replied, "but don't any of you leave the porch."

That's when Joe spoke up, "Mom, John said me and Kevin could come over and watch from his house."

John was in eighth grade at MBS. He was a year older than my brother Joe, two years older than me. John lived on Chester Avenue, just a half-block from 58th Street. At John's house, we'd have an even better view of the protest march.

"No way," Mom said, "you guys aren't going anywhere 'til this is over."

Joe didn't give up, "But Mom, I heard the Bartram kids ain't gonna be here for a while."

"The answer is no," Mom shot back.

That's when I spoke up, "C'mon, Mom, look at all the cops on 58th Street. We'll be walking right past them on our way to John's house."

Mom didn't have an answer for that. She could easily see, right from our front porch, that there was an incredible amount of police near the corner of 58th and Chester Avenue. Not only were there lots of cops from the 12th District, there was also an entire busload of extra cops parked just up from the intersection. There were cops on motorcycles, even cops on horseback. I'd never seen so many cops.

"Alright, you two can go," Mom said, "but you better call me the minute you get to John's house."

As Joe and I walked toward 58th and Chester Avenue, lots of neighbors were lining up on the sidewalk to get a good view of the protest march that was headed our way. When we got to the intersection, I looked up the steps leading to the main entrance into the public church. There, at the top of the steps, were three TV cameramen, one from each of the major TV stations. They had their cameras set up with a great angle to the intersection below.

"Joe, look," I said, pointing up the steps, "TV cameras."

"Cool," Joe said. "Maybe they'll put our neighborhood on the news tonight."

As we walked past all the police, I noticed many of them were just standing around, talking and laughing. Some were drinking coffee and smoking cigarettes. They looked too relaxed. I got the feeling the protest march still had a ways to go before it would get to our area. When we got to John's house, the first thing we did was call Mom. We knew if we didn't call, she'd be calling John's house any second, and she'd probably make us come right home as punishment for not calling her first. From John's front steps, we could see that no one was on the basketball courts at Myers playground, which was a rare sight. But, then again, it wasn't every day that a protest march was headed to our area. So the three of us grabbed a basketball and went over to play a quick game of Utah.

Utah was our favorite game when we only had three players. The two guys who didn't have the ball covered the guy who did. No fouls were called, so the games could get rough. The only reason the games didn't get too rough was because we all knew that if we fouled someone really hard, we'd get fouled even harder when we got the ball.

As soon as we started playing, we heard a voice from up high yell, "Yo guys."

It was Tom McGlone, an undercover Philly cop. He was yelling down from the top of the black fire-escape steps that led up to his second-floor office in the back of Myers gym. His office windows overlooked the outside basketball courts, so he was able to see us right away.

2009 photo of Officer McGlone's office, now boarded up, at top of steps overlooking courts in Myers playground. Photo courtesy of Bill Dorsch.

Tom, as he always told us to call him, continued yelling down to us, "You guys be careful. I just heard on my police radio that the march is about a half-hour away."

About a year earlier, Tom began working out of that office. I'd never seen him before that. I think the Police Department and the Recreation Department got together and set Tom up in that office to keep an eye on all the trouble that was going on around Myers playground. Tom always looked out for us. He was an assistant coach on MBS' football and basketball teams, so he knew us pretty well. Tom looked to be in his late thirties, about 5'10," full head of perfectly parted dark hair, solidly built with powerful arms that looked like granite blocks.

Our friend John yelled back up to Tom, "We're goin' to my house as soon as the march gets here."

Tom yelled back, "I'll give you a holler when it's getting close."

"Thanks, Tom," we all yelled back.

About 20 minutes later, Tom came out of his office and yelled down, "Get out of here. It's getting close." Tom then locked his office door, hurried down the fire escape steps, and broke into a slow jog on his way to the 58th Street side of the playground, where all the other cops were waiting for the protest march to get there.

John told us to follow him. All along, I thought we were going to hang out in front of John's house to watch the protest. But John had another idea. Instead of leading us out of the playground, John took us to a spot under one of the tall trees that lined the Chester Avenue edge of Myers playground. John looked straight up, pointed, and said, "Check this out." As I looked up, I noticed that the tree's branches were perfectly spaced for climbing, like the spacing on a stepladder. I wasn't much of a tree climber, but this looked like a tree even I could climb. All we had to do was scale the six-foot, chain-link fence, grab onto a low-lying limb, pull ourselves up, and start climbing.

John went first, and easily got himself up into the tree. He'd obviously done this before. Me and my brother Joe were right behind him. It was the easiest tree I'd ever climbed. And it was the highest tree I'd ever climbed. We must have been 30 to 40 feet off the ground. So there we sat: me, Joe, and John, with an incredible view of all the cops, all the newsmen, and the hundreds of people from our neighborhood who had lined up on the sidewalk, waiting for the protest march. Within minutes, I could hear the students chanting. I couldn't make out what they were saying, but they didn't sound happy. Once I was able to see them, I couldn't believe it. It was the biggest group of people I'd ever seen on a city street. The next day's *Evening Bulletin* would say there were about 1,000 students in the march.

Street Fighting Erupts Following Bartram Walkout

JUN 13 1970

About 4,000 black students from John Bartram High School and some 400 white students from neighborhood schools engaged in sporadic street fighting yesterday afternoon at 58th st. and Chester av.

There were fist fights and some bottle and brick throwing, police said. About 100 policemen were sent to the area shortly after 3.30 P.M. and within a half hour dispersed crowds that had gathered.

Philadelphia Evening Bulletin, *Newspaper clipping collection.*
Philadelphia, Temple University Libraries, Urban Archives.

As soon as the first group of Bartram students walked past the front of Myers gym, seven Dirty Annies jumped out from the side of the building, throwing bottles and rocks into the crowd. Then those same Dirty Annies ran out onto 58th Street and started fist fighting with some of the Bartram students.

"Holy shit," I said in disbelief, "look at those guys!"

"They're crazy, man," John added, "totally crazy."

Then Joe said, "They're in big trouble now."

In a matter of seconds, about 10 cops surrounded the seven Dirty Annies, handcuffed them, and threw them into one of the police paddy wagons parked nearby.

As the march got closer and closer to 58th and Chester Avenue, where most of the neighborhood people had gathered, tempers got hotter. As loud as the Bartram kids were chanting, a lot of the neighbors tried to outshout them.

"Get the hell out of our neighborhood," I heard one lady yell.

Another woman yelled at the top of her lungs, "You're the ones who started all this."

While both sides were screaming at each other, six more Dirty Annies in the back of the crowd started firing bottles and rocks at the Bartram kids. Then they took off running down Chester Avenue toward 59th Street, with two cop cars racing after them. I heard later that all six of them got locked up, too.

When the Bartram kids passed 58th and Chester Avenue, they kept walking up 58th Street and out of sight. Me, Joe, and John climbed down out of the tree and walked over to the intersection, still packed with police, newsmen, and neighbors.

That's when I heard a familiar voice coming from the top of the church steps saying, "Don't put their pictures on TV, that's what they want."

It was Mom's voice. She was yelling at the TV cameramen. Mom had left my youngest brothers at home with Larry, so she could come down and see for herself what was going on. Me and Joe hurried up the steps to get Mom.

At the same time, a cop was also walking up the steps toward Mom, saying, "Ma'am, you need to calm down."

"No, I'm not calming down," Mom said. She was really upset. "It's not right to put their pictures on TV, that's what they want."

"Listen, lady," the cop said, he was getting pissed off now, "one more word out of you and you're under arrest for inciting a riot."

Me and Joe grabbed Mom by the hands and led her down the church steps. We knew Mom always spoke her mind. And we knew if we didn't get her away, she was headed for trouble. As we walked away with Mom, she was still angry. I don't think I'd ever seen her so angry. It was a deep anger. So deep, I really don't think it had anything to do with the kids from Bartram or the TV cameramen. I got the feeling that Mom was releasing months of frustration about the whole neighborhood situation.

Mom and Dad had worked hard to be able to raise five boys in their own home in what used to be such a great neighborhood. But their home, our home, was now smack in the middle of what was fast becoming one of the most dangerous neighborhoods in all of Philly.

It wasn't that Mom didn't like black people. Neither of our parents taught us to think badly about black people. Once the neighborhood started getting bad, Mom would tell us time and time again, "There are good whites and good blacks. And there are bad whites and bad blacks." Mom was upset about the entire situation, a situation that was steadily getting out of control and starting to put her kids in danger.

That night, we turned on the news to see the protest march on TV. It was cool to see our neighborhood on TV. Our neighborhood was hardly ever on the news. They showed the huge crowd of Bartram students walking down 58th Street. Then they showed some of the fights that broke out along the way. The TV newsman mentioned that Bartram High School was going to be closed on Monday, and that some of the "G" buses were going to be re-routed so they wouldn't pass through our neighborhood. The newsman also said that summer school classes, which were supposed to be held at Bartram High, were going to be relocated to schools up in West Philly so the students wouldn't have to ride buses through our neighborhood. Finally, the news report showed a group of the Dirty Annies hanging out in front of the corner store of the same name. During the news report, the Dirty Annies gang was mentioned over and over for all of Philly to hear.

That summer, the Dirty Annies got into a lot of fights. In August, in a fight near 58th and Warrington Avenue, one of the Dirty Annies got shot. The 18-year-old kid who got shot was one of the kids who used to hang out at The Sunshine Inn, near 58th and Willows Avenue, but was now hanging out at Dirty Annie's.

To get to Dirty Annie's, he had to walk a half-mile from his home through a mostly black section of the neighborhood. Usually, he walked back and forth to Dirty Annie's with some friends who lived near him. But that night, none of those guys were around. So he was going to walk home alone. Some of the Dirty Annies wouldn't let him go alone. They knew it might be dangerous, so they decided they'd walk him home and then walk back to Dirty Annie's.

Just two blocks into their walk up 58th Street, a fight broke out with a gang of black kids. One of the black kids pulled out a gun. The 18-year-old white kid got shot. The bullet entered his lung and exited through his back. With the help of a respirator, doctors were able to save the kid's life.

The next day, when I heard what happened, I couldn't believe it. I couldn't believe a kid actually got shot just a couple blocks from our house. The last thing this neighborhood needed was for guns to be involved.

CHAPTER 9
September, 1970:
Tension at Most Blessed Sacrament (MBS)

EVEN THOUGH THERE'D been a lot of racial trouble in the neighborhood for some time now, the racial situation inside MBS School had remained pretty calm. For the most part, black kids and white kids in MBS got along with each other. But starting in seventh grade, the year I turned 12, I could sense racial tension growing in the school itself and in the streets around the school.

At MBS, we didn't eat lunch at school. We all walked home for lunch. Then we all walked back to MBS for afternoon classes. When we returned to MBS schoolyard after lunch, the scene was total chaos. Even though MBS's enrollment had shrunk from about 3,500 students to about 2,000, the schoolyard was still packed with kids waiting for the afternoon bell to ring. The younger kids would be running around playing tag. Older girls would be jumping rope and playing hopscotch. Older boys would be throwing balls, flipping baseball cards, playing wall-ball, or just hanging out.

Most of the older black kids hung out together in their own corner of the schoolyard. So many black families were moving into our neighborhood, it seemed like there were twice as many black kids in MBS this year compared to the year before. Still, there were never any big fights in the schoolyard between the white kids from MBS and the black kids from MBS. Once in a while, there'd be a one-on-one fight between a white kid and black kid who had an argument. But that was the extent of it. The big fights that were happening now were between the white kids from MBS and the black kids from Mitchell School.

Mitchell School was our neighborhood's public elementary school. It's where I went to kindergarten. Mitchell School was diagonally across the street from MBS, on the corner of 56th and Kingsessing Avenue. At the time, most of the kids who went to Mitchell School were black. A lot of the trouble was happening at lunchtime. When the white kids from MBS walked back to school after lunch, many walked right past Mitchell schoolyard. At that time of day, a lot of the black kids from Mitchell School were hanging out in Mitchell schoolyard for recess. That was never a problem in years past. Now it was a problem. Both groups would yell racial stuff back and forth, and fights began to break out.

My walk back and forth to MBS wasn't anywhere near Mitchell. So me and my brothers weren't directly involved in the trouble at Mitchell until after the fighting started. As soon as a fight broke out with the kids from Mitchell, word quickly spread through MBS schoolyard. Me and my friends would run over to 56th and Kingsessing Avenue to see what was going on. At the same time we were running over to the fight, a lot of black kids from Mitchell schoolyard were also running to the fight. Some of the fights turned into full-blown brawls involving 20 or more kids on each side. Because the fights were happening during school hours, nobody had any weapons, so the fights usually involved just belts and fists. And the fights usually ended quickly as the nuns from MBS and teachers from Mitchell ran over to get things under control.

Whenever we saw the nuns coming, we all tried to look as innocent as possible. Even if we weren't involved in the fight, if certain nuns thought we were guilty, then we were guilty. And that usually meant getting cracked with a wooden yardstick on some part of our body when we got back inside MBS. I remember seeing a nun beat the hell out of a kid who was involved in one of the fights with the kids from Mitchell. The beating happened in the coatroom. I was carrying boxes of supplies for my teacher, so I was allowed to use the elevator, which was all the way in the back of the huge coatroom, an open area big enough to hang the coats of hundreds of seventh-graders. I tried to pretend I wasn't watching, but I saw the whole thing. The nun pushed some coats aside to make room on the metal pole that we hung our coats on. Then she forced the kid to hold on to the metal pole as she whacked him across the back of the legs about six or seven times with a three-sided wooden yardstick. Man, did that look painful. It even sounded painful hearing the kid yell each time he got hit. It just wasn't right. Yet, few kids, if any, would go home and tell their parents that a nun beat the hell out of them. Most parents, including my parents, were of the mind that if we did something bad enough for a nun to beat us up, we deserved to get beat up again when we got home. Luckily, only a few of the nuns were that violent. Most of the nuns were nice people who really cared about the kids. But the few crazy nuns seemed to get way too much pleasure out of beating the hell out of young kids. It wasn't unusual to see those nuns slapping kids across the face, both boys and girls, for small stuff like chewing gum or not paying attention during class. And it wasn't a gentle slap. It was a hard slap, the kind that left finger marks on the side of the kid's face. Those were the nuns we all tried to steer clear of.

As more and more fights kept breaking out between the white kids from MBS and the black kids from Mitchell, the cops got involved. Before long, cop cars were stationed at every intersection near both schools in the morning, at lunchtime, and after school. That quickly put an end to most of those fights.

That same year, in seventh grade, I began to notice changes in my relationships with some of the black friends I'd made over the years. Some black kids at MBS that I'd known for years started to act like they didn't even know me anymore. One day, I was walking down the hallway between classes when I saw Kenny walking toward me. Kenny was a black kid I'd known for about three years. We were never real close. But we always got along, and said "hi" to each other. Kenny was walking toward me with two other black kids who were new to MBS. I didn't know the new kids at all.

"Hey Kenny," I said as we passed each other in the hall.

Recently, I'd noticed that whenever Kenny was with these new kids, he was acting kind of cold toward me. This time, he just ignored me. When he heard me say his name, he turned toward me. Then he quickly snapped his head right back to make it look like he didn't see me.

At first, I wasn't sure why Kenny was trying to ignore me. Then I figured it might have something to do with all the new black kids in MBS. I had a feeling a lot of the new black kids were putting pressure on the black kids who'd been at MBS for a while. They didn't want them to be so friendly with white kids anymore. I know I was feeling more and more pressure from some of the tougher white kids to stop being friendly with black kids. Nobody ever said anything to me about it. But sometimes, if I was talking to a black friend in school, I noticed some of the white kids would give me dirty looks. Still, it pissed me off that Kenny couldn't even give me a nod or something. The next time I saw him, I totally ignored him, and I never said a word to him again. I figured two could play that game.

Outside of school, even my relationship with my friend Dwight was changing. Dwight's the black kid I was friends with when we used to play basketball together at Myers playground. One afternoon, five of us were walking along Chester Avenue. It was me, Joe, Larry, and our friends Chris and Donny. At the same time, five black kids about our age were walking straight toward us. When the black kids got closer, I noticed one of them was Dwight. I hardly ever saw Dwight anymore. That was the first time I'd seen him in months.

One of Dwight's friends was carrying a huge boom-box on his right shoulder. In almost every crowd of black kids walking the streets, one of them was usually carrying a boom-box. And it was usually blasting WDAS, a Philly radio station that played black music. Dwight's friend's boom-box was so big it was pushing in the right side of his afro as he balanced it on his shoulder.

His boom-box was blasting The Temptations' new hit, a song called "Ball of Confusion." The song began with the words, *"People movin' out, people movin' in. Why, because of the color of their skin. Run, run, run, but you sure can't hide."* Every time I heard that song, I felt like The Temptations were singing about our neighborhood.

Some of my friends hated those boom-boxes. Sometimes they'd yell at the black kids walking by, telling them to turn their music down. I didn't mind the loud music at all. I actually enjoyed it. As much as I liked the music of The Beatles and The Stones, I liked the music of The Temptations, Jackson 5, and Sly and the Family Stone every bit as much.

As me and my friends got closer to Dwight and his friends, I didn't think there would be a fight. Neither of our groups that afternoon had anyone with us who liked to start trouble. Still, any time a group of white kids walked past a group of black kids there was tension in the air. When our groups passed each other on a narrow stretch of sidewalk, neither group gave up any ground. So there was the usual shoulder-to-shoulder bumping that often led to a fight. But this time, both groups kept walking.

I briefly made eye contact with Dwight. Recently, I'd been trying my best to avoid eye contact with black kids I'd pass on the street. I'd try to walk with my head down and my eyes up. In the past, especially when I was alone, I noticed that whenever my eyes met the eyes of certain black kids, they took it as a challenge.

"Who you looking at?" some of them would say. And I'd find myself getting into a fight. I figured if I kept my eyes to myself, I could avoid a lot of trouble. It usually worked.

Dwight was an exception. I still considered Dwight a friend. As we passed each other, I briefly looked his way. We both gave each other a little nod that none of our friends noticed. It was as if both of us were acknowledging each other, knowing we don't dare say a word to each other in these kinds of situations anymore. If talk got around that I was being friendly with black kids on the street, I could get punched in the face by some of the tougher white kids in our neighborhood.

Walking past Dwight that day was another one of those moments when I thought to myself: Whatever this black and white stuff is all about, it just doesn't make any sense. But it's the way it is now. And I'm just gonna have to play the game.

CHAPTER 10
May, 1971:
Murder in Cobbs Creek Park

COBBS CREEK PARK is a huge park that forms a big part of the border between Southwest Philly and the surrounding suburbs. The park was close to Myers playground, just a three-block walk from the playground entrance near 59th and Chester Avenue. Having the park so close by was really cool. Even though we lived in a crowded city, we could be in the middle of the woods in a matter of minutes. The park always seemed so peaceful compared to the busy city streets. So it was even more tragic when such a peaceful place became the scene of a gang fight that cost a kid his life.

Because Cobbs Creek Park was so close by, lots of people from our neighborhood would walk over to play ball, have picnics, walk the stepping-stones across the creek, explore the woods, that kind of stuff. In the winter, when temperatures dropped below freezing, a lot of people would ice skate on the frozen creek. The park also had some great hills for sledding. One of the park's steepest hills was called the "nutcracker." When my brother Joe was 10, he broke his leg sledding down the nutcracker. Given the name of the hill, I guess it could have been worse.

When we were younger, Dad used to take me and my brothers to the park to teach us how to play baseball. He'd teach us how to hit, how to catch fly balls, and how to field ground balls. I especially remember being at the park one hot, June afternoon when I was just five years old. I remember it was Father's Day. We played baseball for about an hour. On our walk home, Dad stopped at the gas station across the street from the park to buy us each a cold soda. When the man working at the gas station was getting our sodas, Dad could hear that the transistor radio in the gas station was tuned to the Phillies game. So Dad asked the man, "How'd the Phillies do in the first game?"

The Phillies were playing a doubleheader against the Mets that day. Dad was hoping to get back home in time to watch the second game.

"Didn't you hear?" the man said. "Jim Bunning pitched a perfect game."

"You're kidding me, right?" Dad asked as his eyes widened like he'd just seen a ghost.

"He really did it," the man reassured Dad, "he pitched a perfect game."

Because I was only five at the time, I had no idea what a perfect game was. But I could tell from how excited Dad was, a perfect game must have been something special. Years later, when I learned how rare a perfect game is, I appreciated Dad's facial expression that day even more.

As our neighborhood got more and more dangerous, Cobbs Creek Park became popular for a different kind of activity, underage drinking. In years past, I'd see teenagers drinking bottles of beer and bottles of wine in brown paper bags right on the street corners. These days, way too many cops were circling the area. It was rare if two or three minutes passed without a cop car cruising by. With so many cops around, drinking on the street corners became too risky. So, on weekends, lots of teenagers, black and white, went to Cobbs Creek Park to drink. I began hearing stories of fights breaking out at the park on weekends. And on one particular Friday night, when the fighting started, things got out of hand.

Stepping-stones in Cobbs Creek Park, scene of a gang-related stabbing death.

According to the next day's *Bulletin*, just after 10 o'clock, about 10 to 15 Dirty Annies were drinking beer on one side of Cobbs Creek, while seven black guys were drinking beer on the other side. When the two groups spotted each other, they started yelling racial stuff back and forth.

The *Bulletin* article said that one of the black guys began walking across the stepping-stones toward the other side of the creek where the Dirty Annies were drinking. Some of the Dirty Annies chased him back. One of the Dirty Annies had a Boy Scout knife. A fight broke out and one of the black guys was stabbed in the stomach, arms, and left shoulder. By the time he arrived at the hospital, he was dead at the age of 20.

I found out about the murder the next day. We were eating lunch at the Vittle Vat: me, my brother Joe, and our friends John and Chris. The Vittle Vat was a narrow store, so narrow its one-person-at-a-time front door took up about one-third of the entire storefront. The other two-thirds had a big window where people walking by could see and smell the cheesesteaks being cooked. Inside the Vittle Vat, just past the main counter on the left and the large soda refrigerator on the right, four steps led down to a dining room with about eight wooden tables and chairs. The dining room was a great place to eat lunch, drink a soda, or just hang out. I spent time in the Vittle Vat's dining room almost every day. I liked all the Vittle Vat's sandwiches, especially their cheesesteaks.

A few weeks before the murder in the park, the Vittle Vat cut back on the hours that customers could sit in the dining room. Two Dirty Annies got caught down there huffing model airplane glue out of brown-paper bags. They usually got the glue from Dirty Annie's store, but they didn't buy the glue themselves. Word was getting around that a few guys in the neighborhood were huffing the glue to get high. So Dirty Annie's store wouldn't sell the glue by itself anymore. The glue had to be bought together with a model. The guys who wanted to huff the glue would never go into the store themselves and buy a model. That would look too suspicious. So they would get kids my age to buy it for them. It never happened to me, but it did happen to one of my friends.

One of the older guys asked him if he wanted a model airplane for free. My friend said yes. So the older guy gave him the money and told him to make sure he bought some model glue with the airplane. Then the older guy told my friend he could keep the model, but he had to give the older guy the glue. He said he needed the glue for some of his models at home.

One afternoon, I saw one of the Dirty Annies huffing glue while I was sitting in the Vittle Vat's dining room, eating lunch with a couple friends. The kid was sitting at the table furthest in the back, in a seat against the wall. Every few minutes, he'd bury his head into a small, brown-paper lunch bag with its sides rolled down about one-third of the way. When the kid's head would come back up out of the bag, he looked like a zombie. His face was beet red. His eyes looked like they were about to roll into the back of their sockets. And he seemed like he had no idea what was going on.

It didn't look like a lot of fun. I mean, I'd seen lots of older guys drinking beer and smoking pot. They looked like they were feeling good and having fun. Seeing them made me want to try drinking beer and smoking pot when I got older. But when I saw that kid huffing glue, I decided right then and there, there was no way I was ever going near that stuff. In fact, even though I didn't build many models, seeing that kid huffing glue that day made me never want to build a model again if it meant having that glue anywhere near me.

Anyway, that's where I was when I heard about the murder in Cobbs Creek Park, sitting downstairs in the Vittle Vat with my brother Joe, and our friends John and Chris.

"Do they know who did it?" I asked.

John replied, "Nobody's saying. But everyone thinks some of the Dirty Annies were involved."

"Nuts, isn't it?" Chris said.

I felt bad that the black kid got killed. The newspaper the next day would say he was a hard-working kid from a big family. I couldn't imagine what it would be like if one of my brothers or one of my friends got killed. And I hoped I'd never have to find out. But as bad as I felt for the kid who got killed, I was also thinking about the murder's impact on us.

"We'd better watch our asses," I said, "some of these guys are gonna be out for revenge."

Our table got real quiet as we all kept eating. It was like the seriousness of the murder was beginning to sink in. The more I thought about it, the more I thought about how fights in our neighborhood were no longer between individuals. Years ago, most of the fights I'd see were one against one. Now it was gang against gang. And, as I'd seen so many times watching the Dirty Annies fight, when it's gang against gang, anything goes.

Every gang had some kids who liked to start trouble. And the Dirty

Annies were no exception. But most of the Dirty Annies I knew were really nice guys. Still, even the nicest guys, the guys who usually didn't get into fights, would get sucked into the "all for one, one for all" mentality once a gang fight started.

Four Dirty Annies were arrested for the murder in Cobbs Creek Park. According to the *Bulletin*, they were caught later that night riding around in a car near 57th and Springfield Avenue. The kid who did the stabbing was sentenced to three to 10 years in prison. The other kids got probation.

4 Held in Cobbs Creek Park Killing

Philadelphia Evening Bulletin, *Newspaper clipping collection.*
Philadelphia, Temple University Libraries, Urban Archives.

Of the four Dirty Annies arrested, only one still lived in our neighborhood at the time of the murder. The other three had already moved out to the suburbs. That was another crazy thing about our neighborhood. As dangerous as it was getting, many white kids who had already moved out kept coming back weekend after weekend. I really believe it had a lot to do with the strong bonds that were formed growing up together in a neighborhood like ours. Kids in our neighborhood looked out for each other and fought for each other in a way that most kids from safer neighborhoods never had to. When kids from our neighborhood moved out, they missed those bonds. So it wasn't surprising that so many of them came back every weekend. And it also wasn't surprising that so many of them had to *sneak* back. Nobody's parents wanted their kids coming back to the dangerous neighborhood they'd worked so hard to move out of. But they did come back, every weekend, taking buses, els, and trolleys to be back in Southwest Philly hanging out with their boys.

The murder in Cobbs Creek Park was all over the news. Before our neighborhood started getting dangerous, the only part of the newspaper I ever looked at was the sports section. Now, every day, I looked through every page of both the *Bulletin* and the *Inquirer*, searching for articles about what was going on in our neighborhood. And there was a lot going on.

Around the same time of the murder in the park, in a fight near 56th and Greenway Avenue, a 16-year-old white kid got stabbed in the chest by a black kid. Doctors said the white kid would have died if the cut were inches closer to his heart.

Also, around the same time, near 58th and Chester Avenue, a 14-year-old white kid got into a fight with a 14-year-old black kid. The white kid ended up hitting the black kid in the head with a broom handle. The black kid died.

A lot of kids carried broom handles. We used them as baseball bats when we played half-ball. Half-balls were air balls that had gone flat. We'd cut the flat air balls in half with a penknife and stack them together. The pitcher would toss the half-balls underhanded to the batter who tried to hit them with the broom handle. Some of the best half-ball players took the sport very seriously, customizing their broom handles by sawing one end for a perfect length and taping the other end for a better grip.

Most cops would let us carry our broom handles. They saw us playing half-ball a lot, so they knew we used them as baseball bats. I guess the cops figured that if they took our broom handles from us, it would be like they were taking a piece of sporting equipment from us. But broom handles were more than just a piece of sporting equipment once a fight broke out. They became a weapon, and a very good weapon. The kids who got hit with broom handles usually got hurt pretty bad. Unfortunately, that day, when the two 14-year-olds got into a fight, the broom handle became a fatal weapon.

The 14-year-old white kid was sentenced to a few years in a juvenile detention center. An article in the *Bulletin* said the 14-year-old black kid who got killed had just moved into our neighborhood from another dangerous area in South Philly, near 30th and Tasker, where white kids and black kids were fighting a lot. The article said the black kid's family moved to our neighborhood because they thought it would be a safer place to live.

Our neighborhood was mentioned in the newspapers just about every day. And the biggest stories were about the Dirty Annies gang. One Sunday, the *Inquirer* ran a long feature story about the gang right on the front page of its local section. The reporter quoted a lot of the Dirty Annies who didn't want their names in the paper. Almost all of them talked about having to fight to protect the only territory they had left in the neighborhood.

One Dirty Annie said, "If we don't stick together, we're going to get killed. It's their [the blacks'] neighborhood now."

The Philadelphia Inquirer

SUNDAY MORNING, MAY 16, 1971

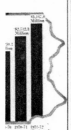

on Time in Debt

. a situation that cannot orge Thompson must learn nany of the things he is

or George Thompson, he

for the taxpayers of Penn- n get an accurate picture adding five zeroes to the ompson's figures.

INNING

wealth borrows money for : reason that individuals mpson borrow money — nediately the benefits of be paid for immediately. fe it needs things when it

and 1966, state publicists bout "record" numbers of ge 10, Col. 1

).A. Weighs itate Probe of Iillcrest Death

By KEN SHUTTLEWORTH
Of The Inquirer Staff
HONESDALE.—The State ustice Department may be

Plan Offered To Cut Cost Of Divorce

Bar Suggestions Would Reduce Tab To Less Than $100

By ANTHONY LAME
Of The Inquirer Staff

The Family Court Division of Philadelphia's court system will launch a study soon of nine recommendations designed to streamline procedure in divorce cases and lower the cost of divorce suits.

The recommendations include:

—SETTING THE COST of filing a divorce suit at $12.

—REDUCING THE FEE of the court—appointed master who has jurisdiction in a case —from $129 to $80.

—ABOLITION of the $15 fee that a plaintiff is currently required to pay to the Philadelphia Bar Association.

—SHORTENING the master's report and substituting depositions and affidavits for costly and unnecessary investigation by the court-appointed master.

The recommendations were made in a report by the bar association's special committee on the mastership system and divorce proceedings, chaired by Nochem Winnet, former county court judge.

The report has been approved by the bar association's board of governors, but the specific recommendations require the approval of the board of judges of Common Pleas Court before they may be implemented.

APPOINTS LAWYER

Frank Montemuro administrative judge of the Family Court, said he has appointed a panel of 10 family court judges to study the recommendations and advise the board of judges on whether to adopt them. The Family Court has jurisdiction over all divorce proceedings.

Under the mastership system, the family court appoints a lawyer, who is called a

Robin Hood Dell to Get A New Home in the Park

Inquirer photo by EARNEST S. EDDOWES
Dirty Annies at a Favorite Corner, 58th and Chester
They feel defensive; and many don't hide racial animosity

White Gang Is Resentful Of 'Takeover' in Area

By THOMAS J. MADDEN
Of The Inquirer Staff

They took their name from a little candy store at Alden and Chester which they nicknamed "Dirty Annie's."

They claim they are not a "gang"—only a "group" of

★ ★ ★

Background

Myers Recreation Center at 58th and Kingsessing ave. and other parts of Southwest Philadelphia have become battlegrounds between black youths and the Dirty Annies, a white "gang."

Roofed Center For 6000 Will Cost $9 Million

By GERALD ETTER
Of The Inquirer Staff

Robin Hood Dell—haven for music lovers since 1930 — will find a new home in Fairmount Park, giving Philadelphia a summer center for the performing arts.

Plans are scheduled to be announced this week for the project which will cost close to $9 million and accommodate 6000 people under a roof.

The announcement will be made by Robin Hood Dell president Fredric R. Mann, who has headed the operation for 22 years.

FREDRIC MANN

Mann had, in the past, often discussed plans for moving the concert setting elsewhere in the park.

"If the Bicentennial Commission can rouse the interest of the government," he had said, "then it might be possible to point out the need to build a permanent covered building in the park."

This week's announcement is expected to reveal the basic plans for the new Dell along with a demonstration model and anticipated costs.

Though complete financing for the project has not been promised, it is believed the sponsors will seek funding aid from such organizations as the Ford Foundation.

The building will go up on a site across the Schuylkill from the present Dell amphi-

'Dirty Annies' Stick Together: 'If We Don't, We're Dead, It's a Black Section Now'

Another Dirty Annie said, "White parents are starting to realize they've got to help us out. We're the last white gang."

One other Dirty Annie added something similar about how the changing neighborhood had changed the attitude of a lot of white adults.

"The white adults," he said, "never used to like us; now a lot of them are behind us. Last night me and two other kids were standing on the corner when a group of blacks came by. A lady invited us on her porch as they went by. That never happened before. They used to let us fend for ourselves."

An article in the *Evening Bulletin* told the black people's side of the story. A black woman was quoted as saying, "This was once a predominantly white neighborhood and then the blacks moved in. The whites are against it. They're so much against it, they'll just do anything."

Later in the story, a black man was quoted as saying, "These are the poor whites, with no place to go. They're making their last stand to keep from being forced out and that's what created this situation of bigotry and prejudice."

That second quote had a lot of truth to it. The Dirty Annies were the last white gang their age in our neighborhood, and they weren't going to be forced out. In fact, they were more determined than ever to protect what little territory they had left. We all were. As the number of us white people kept shrinking, it seemed as if the bonds among those of us who remained kept getting stronger and stronger. We knew that there weren't a whole lot of us left, and we all had to stick together.

Even on TV, the murder in Cobbs Creek Park was a big story. And the Dirty Annies were the biggest part of the story. One TV news report showed the scene of the murder in Cobbs Creek Park, then cut to a shot of a group of Dirty Annies hanging out on the corner. The murder in the park made the Dirty Annies one of the most talked-about gangs in all of Philly. And it made the streets in our neighborhood more dangerous than ever.

CHAPTER 11
June, 1971:
Strength in Numbers

EVER SINCE THE murder in Cobbs Creek Park, I could feel the racial tension throughout the neighborhood growing stronger and stronger. The *Bulletin* ran some articles about community leaders holding meetings with parents and teenagers, black and white, to try to calm things down.

But things didn't calm down. One day I heard that a black guy in a slow-moving car pointed a gun out the window at a group of Dirty Annies who were hanging out on their corner. No shots were fired, but the threat was loud and clear.

A few days later, something like that happened to us when we were hanging out in the corner of Myers playground near 59th and Chester Avenue. I didn't know if he had a gun or not, but a black guy in a slow-moving car leaned out of the front passenger window and, using both hands, pointed a metal object at us. A couple of my friends yelled, "Gun! Gun!" I dove to the ground, as did most of the guys I was with. Again, no shots were fired.

The only thing keeping us safe was all the police in the area. Everywhere I looked, I saw either a cop car cruising by, or a couple of cops walking the beat. Both were welcome sights.

Our little corner of Myers playground, near 59th and Chester Avenue, was the only part of the playground where we could still hang out. Black kids were now hanging out on the basketball courts and every other part of the playground, even near the Old House. We were more outnumbered than ever before, especially now that more white kids than ever had gone down to the Jersey shore for the summer. A lot of our oldhead got jobs in Wildwood. Then there was the usual group of guys who went down the shore every summer with their families. And this year, a few of the guys, including my friend Chris, were sent away for the summer to live with relatives. Chris was spending the summer with his cousins down the shore. A lot of parents were trying to find any way possible to get their kids out of this neighborhood that was getting more and more dangerous by the day. Because so few of us were hanging out in our little corner of Myers playground, we would often get attacked by black kids throwing rocks and bottles. We'd fight back for a while. But we were usually so outnumbered we'd have to retreat down Chester Avenue toward 60th Street, which was still a mostly white area. It was easy to see that Myers playground was not going to be a safe place to hang out that summer.

At that time, there was one other group of white kids about our age who were still hanging out in the neighborhood. They used to hang out near 55th and Kingsessing Avenue, but that was getting too dangerous. So they started hanging out near 56th Street, in MBS schoolyard. When we found out those guys were now hanging out in MBS schoolyard, we started hanging out there, too. Most of the guys in the other group were a couple of years older than me, but younger than most of the Dirty Annies. I didn't know those guys very well. But I know I sure felt safer hanging out in a bigger group.

Another good thing about hanging out in MBS schoolyard: we were still just a block away from the Dirty Annies. It was always comforting to know the Dirty Annies were close-by, although a lot of them had gone down the shore for the summer, too.

MBS' property was like a stone fortress that took up most of the area between 56th Street and 57th Street, from Kingsessing Avenue to Chester Avenue. MBS Church sat like a palace on the corner of 56th and Chester Avenue. The crosses at the top of the church's two green domes were so high, they looked down over the entire neighborhood. MBS' two domes could easily be seen from blocks away in every direction. Sometimes me and my brothers would skip Mass and go over to Myers playground to hang out until Mass was over. Even from the playground, more than two blocks from MBS, I could see the crucifixes at the top of the church's two domes. I knew my parents wouldn't find out that we were skipping Mass. But the sight of those crucifixes looking down over us reminded me that God knew. I felt guilty, but I figured I'd just go to Confession, admit I skipped Mass, say a couple extra "Our Fathers," and everything would be cool again.

MBS Church in center, rectory on right, school buildings on left.
Philadelphia Evening Bulletin, *Photojournalism collection.*
Philadelphia, Temple University Libraries, Urban Archives.

I didn't like going to Confession. I never understood why I had to tell another human being my sins, instead of just telling God directly. When I'd walk into church on a Saturday afternoon to go to Confession, there were usually at least four priests hearing confessions. So I had to decide which priest I wanted to hear my confession, then I had to get in line to see him. There was definitely a direct relationship between who the priest hearing confessions was and the length of the line waiting to see him. Monsignor Dooley's line was always the shortest. Many times no one was in Monsignor's line even though other priests had lines of 10 people or more. We all knew that, no matter how many sins we confessed, Monsignor would make us say the Stations of the Cross as penance. Having to say the Stations of the Cross meant having to say three different prayers at 14 different locations in the church, which easily took up an extra half-hour on a Saturday afternoon. Most of the other priests only made us say a total of four or five prayers. In a matter of minutes, we'd be back out on the street with our friends enjoying the rest of our Saturday. As much as I didn't like going to Confession, I have to admit, I always felt better afterward. As soon as I walked out of MBS Church, I felt like I had a clean slate.

One of the domes from MBS Church, as seen from Myers playground.
Photo courtesy of Bill Dorsch.

MBS Church was in a huge building, big enough to house two churches, a magnificent large church on the main floor and a second smaller church in the basement. On Sunday mornings, when I was younger, it wasn't unusual for both churches to have standing room only at the same time. Attached to MBS Church on the Chester Avenue side of MBS' property was a three-story, stone rectory where the parish priests lived. Along the 56th Street side of the property were two stone school buildings. One was four stories high. The other was three stories high. Attached to the three-story building was a three-story annex building that was added on when I was younger and nearly 3,500 kids went to school at MBS. Along the Kingsessing Avenue side of MBS property was a four-story, stone convent. About 40 nuns used to live in that convent back when there were so many kids to teach. Now, there couldn't have been more than 20 nuns living there.

MBS schoolyard in 2009. Annex steps, our hangout, are on right.
Photo courtesy of Bill Dorsch.

I definitely felt a lot safer hanging out in MBS schoolyard compared to Myers playground, and not just because we were in a bigger group. At Myers playground, we stood out like a sore thumb, surrounded by black kids who didn't want us hanging out there anymore. At MBS schoolyard, I just felt safer being surrounded by all those huge buildings. Still, even though I felt safer, I knew a lot of black kids were hanging out near MBS schoolyard who didn't want us there, either. At least in the schoolyard, we couldn't see them, and they couldn't see us.

Just like at Myers playground, cops were constantly circling the area near MBS schoolyard. Every hour or so, a cop car would drive through the schoolyard to see what we were up to. Having so many cops around stopped a lot of fights before they could get started. Lots of times, just as a fight was about to break out, a cop car would appear, and both sides would try to innocently walk away, like nothing was happening. Because there were so many cops around, we'd only get into fights about once or twice a week. And that was fine with me. The less fights we had, the better. I just wanted to hang out, play cards, and have fun.

Some of the guys really liked to fight. We had a few guys who would wander away from MBS schoolyard, trying to find black kids to fight with, which wasn't hard to do considering we were pretty much surrounded by them. One of those guys who liked to get fights started was Billy. Billy was a year older than me. He got bored just hanging out. He liked action.

One afternoon, five of us, Billy included, were hanging out on Chester Avenue near MBS schoolyard, eating ice cream and drinking sodas from the ice cream store across the street. While we were standing on the corner, we noticed that two black kids, about our age, were walking toward us. Both kids were strutting the way most black kids in the neighborhood strutted, both arms swinging, one at a time, from about a foot outside their hips to about a foot behind the back of their butt.

It was kind of ironic, but it looked to me like a lot of us white guys were starting to walk with struts, too. I know I started walking with a strut. I started doing it when I noticed the black kids who were strutting had an advantage during the shoulder-to-shoulder bumps when I'd pass them on the sidewalk. Whenever I bumped shoulders with a black kid who was strutting, I usually got the worst of it because he had some momentum in his swinging arms. So I decided that whenever I was walking toward a group of black kids, I was going to walk with a strut, too. I wanted to have some momentum of my own when we made contact. It definitely helped.

As these two black kids strutted closer and closer toward the five of us, I kept thinking to myself, I know Billy's gonna say something. Even though there was a cop car parked just a half-block away, I knew Billy wouldn't let a chance to stir the pot go to waste.

Sure enough, just as the two kids passed us, Billy says, "Cut the strut, niggers."

The two black kids, seeing they were outnumbered, ignored Billy and kept walking. Billy didn't go after the kids because of the cop car parked nearby. I often wondered what made guys like Billy want to start trouble. Did they just like to fight? Was there a lot of violence in their homes? One thing I will say about Billy: he wasn't like some kids in the neighborhood who would start a fight hoping everybody else would finish the fight for them. Whenever Billy started a fight, he always stayed and fought until the end. And Billy was a tough fighter with a powerful punch.

No matter who started the fights, we all got involved. One night, I think there were six of us sitting on the steps of the annex building in the center of MBS schoolyard. Four of us were playing pinochle. The other two guys were working on tricks with their yo-yos. That summer, just about everybody in our crowd had a yo-yo. Yo-yos were the latest fad. I had a yo-yo, but I wasn't very good with mine. The guys who practiced a lot could make their yo-yos do some cool tricks.

On this particular night, just after dark, Father McMurtry's car pulled into MBS schoolyard and into a parking spot near the rectory. Father McMurtry was recently transferred to serve at MBS parish. He was really cool for a priest. He looked like he was in his late thirties or early forties. He had a youthfulness and sincerity about him that helped him connect with us from the get-go. We could tell Father McMurtry was the real deal. In the short time he'd been at MBS, he already knew what was going on in the streets better than all the other priests combined. He would often walk the streets in both the white sections and the black sections of the neighborhood, introducing himself to total strangers. I could tell he wanted to get to the root of what was going on, so he could make a difference in the streets, not just in the church. Unlike a lot of other priests, Father McMurtry made us feel comfortable when he was around. He was always so calm, even when things going on around him were anything but calm.

That night, after Father McMurtry parked his car, he walked over to see us before heading into the rectory for the night. Father McMurtry was wearing what he usually wore: black shoes, black pants, and a black, short-sleeve, button-down shirt with a white collar peeking out near his Adam's apple. Just as we all finished saying our hellos, we heard Billy yelling from up near Kingsessing Avenue, "Yo guys, fight, fight, come on!"

"Wait," Father McMurtry said, "you guys stay here. I'll take care of it."

Father McMurtry took off running toward Kingsessing Avenue. He was in good shape, so he was running pretty fast. As soon as he left us, we all grabbed some bottles and broom handles we'd hidden in a corner of the schoolyard. We always tried to have some weapons handy. Then, we all sprinted up to Kingsessing Avenue, running right past Father McMurtry along the way.

"Guys, stay here. I'll take care of it," he pleaded, as we all ran past him to get to the fight.

We weren't being disrespectful to Father McMurtry. We all respected him. It was just that our friends were in a fight. And we had to help. By now, fighting for each other had become second nature, an impulse. We didn't even think about it. Whenever any of our guys were in a fight, we all ran to help.

We got to the scene of the fight just in time. Billy and three of our friends were outnumbered. When the six of us got to the fight, the numbers evened out. We began fighting with belts, broom handles, car antennas, and bottles right in the middle of Kingsessing Avenue as traffic came to a stop in both directions.

It reminded me of watching the Dirty Annies fighting out in front of our house a few years earlier. Only now, as I suspected then, I was part of the action. But the difference was night and day. Watching street fights out our front window was scary, but I knew I was safe. Being out there in the street in the middle of a gang fight, I wasn't safe.

My first couple experiences in street fights, I tried to act like I was going to hurt someone, but deep down I didn't want to hit anybody. I think, by nature, I was a lot like my dad; I just wanted everyone to get along.

But my mindset changed fast. It had to. When I saw up-close the crazed looks on kids' faces, black and white, during those fights, I knew I had to get tougher. This was no place to be timid. These guys really wanted to hurt each other. And if I didn't develop that same attitude, I was the one who was going to get hurt.

In a way, it was a lot like when I first learned to play tackle football. Eventually I learned that I either hit, or I get hit. There was no in-between. Slowly, but surely, I developed that same attitude on the streets. I started to feel good about whacking somebody with my belt, stick, or car antenna. Because, just like in football, I had to do my part to help my guys beat the other guys.

When Father McMurtry got to where we were fighting, he ran into the middle of Kingsessing Avenue with both arms fully extended, trying to create enough space between our two groups so he could stop the fight. Everyone kept fighting like he wasn't even there. I was concerned that he might get hurt since he was the only one in the street without a weapon of some kind. After about a minute of some intense fighting, we heard the police sirens getting closer, so we took off running back to the schoolyard. Father McMurtry stayed behind to talk with the cops.

When we got back together on the steps of the annex building, our adrenalin was still pumping from the fight.

"George, you got that mother-fucker good," I said, as I patted him on the back with congratulations. George was one of the tougher guys in our crowd. He almost always won his one-on-one battle in our street fights.

"Yeah, he wasn't expectin' me to rush him," said George. "Once I got him on the ground I just kept punchin' him in the face."

"My shoulder's fuckin' killin' me," said Donny, in obvious pain, his left hand reaching around to the back of his right shoulder.

"What happened?" Billy asked.

"One of them mother-fuckers got me on the back of my shoulder with a fuckin' antenna. It's killin' me. Is it bleedin'?"

I carefully lifted the back of Donny's shirt to take a look. "No blood, Donny," I said, "But you got a pretty bad welt."

Then my brother Joe interrupted, "Cops. Everyone be cool."

I looked up and saw a cop car driving into the schoolyard, heading our way. Four of us quickly sat down in a circle as Joe started dealing the pinochle cards he had in his pocket. Donny stopped holding his shoulder. And we all tried to get our adrenaline under control. It was time to act innocent, which we'd gotten pretty good at in recent years.

The cop car pulled right up to us, close enough so the cop could talk to us without having to get out of his car. "What happened up there?" asked the cop.

Billy replied, "Up where?"

"Don't play dumb with me," the cop said, "You guys were just fightin' up on Kingsessing Avenue."

"I don't know what you're talkin' about," said Billy. "We've been here playing cards all night."

"Yeah, right," the cop said. "Don't let me catch you guys startin' any shit. I'll be watchin' you." And then he drove away.

As the cop drove away, Father McMurtry was walking toward us on his way back from the fight scene. "Everybody all right?" asked Father McMurtry.

We all assured him we were OK, even though Donny was still rubbing the back of his shoulder.

"Good," said Father McMurtry as he kept walking toward the rectory. "You guys be careful goin' home later. Good night."

"Good night, Father," we all replied.

As Father McMurtry walked to the rectory, I got to thinking that a lot of priests in his situation would have reamed us out for not listening to them. But Father McMurtry didn't want to cast blame or try to make us feel guilty. He just wanted to know if everybody was all right. Father McMurtry had already figured out that fighting was now a part of life around here. And as long as everybody was OK at the end of the day, it was a good day.

Even though Donny's shoulder got whacked, no one got seriously hurt in that fight. We were lucky that no one got seriously hurt that entire summer. A couple guys had to get some stitches, and we all got our share of bumps and bruises. But that was it.

During that summer, there were times I found myself thinking about our situation compared to what I used to think our lives would be like as 12-year-olds. I expected we'd all be playing in summer baseball and basketball leagues at Myers playground every night. I expected we'd all be hanging out in the playground with a big group of guys and girls, flirting with each other and doing other normal stuff most kids our age were doing. I never expected this. I never expected that all the baseball and basketball summer leagues at Myers playground would be cancelled because of all the racial trouble. I never expected that we'd have nowhere to even play basketball anymore. Every time we tried to play on the outside courts at Myers, we'd get attacked. So we didn't even bother trying. Man, did I miss playing basketball.

As far as hanging out with lots of girls, forget it. There were hardly any girls around anymore. Not long ago, lots of great-looking girls our age lived in this neighborhood. Sometimes on weekends, we'd go to parties at one of the girls' houses. All the boys would hang out on one side of the basement. All the girls would hang out on the other side, closest to the record player so they could keep changing records as they played one hit song after another. I missed hanging out with the big crowd of girls, trying to work up the nerve to talk to the girls I thought were cute. Unfortunately, once the neighborhood started getting dangerous, it seemed like a lot of the families with girls moved out first. Of the few girls who still lived in our neighborhood, some hung out in safer neighborhoods in Southwest Philly, usually in Good Shepherd or Saint Barnabas parishes. Their parents would drive them over there and drop them off, then go back later to pick them up. We didn't like the idea that some of our girls were now hanging out with guys from other parishes. But who could blame them? I know if I were the father of one of those girls I wouldn't want them hanging out in our neighborhood. There were, however, about four or five girls who did hang out with us in MBS schoolyard. Two of them lived less than a block away from the schoolyard. We'd always keep an eye on them to make sure they got home safe. The other girls, who lived farther away, would meet up with some of the guys who lived near them so they could walk to and from the schoolyard together.

Just a couple years ago, I never would have imagined the situation we were in now. One of the nuns at MBS was convinced that, in her words, "When things go bad in life, we're being punished by God for things we did wrong." Sometimes I wondered if maybe she was right. Maybe we were living in this dangerous neighborhood as some kind of punishment for something bad we did in the past. But whenever those kinds of thoughts ran through my mind, I tried as hard as I could to just let them go. Deep down I knew we were simply victims of circumstance. We were the wrong age, in the wrong place, at the wrong time.

Still, despite all the trouble, we had a great time together that summer. I couldn't wait to get together every night in the schoolyard. We didn't sit around worrying about whether or not we were going to get in a fight. We had our weapons on us or nearby: belts, antennas, broom handles, and bottles. If a fight broke out, we were ready, and we'd fight. And if no fight broke out, we just kept hanging out: playing cards, smoking cigarettes, talking sports, and enjoying another fun summer night together in MBS schoolyard.

CHAPTER 12
July, 1971:
Stolen Childhood

ALL THE DANGER in our neighborhood was taking a huge toll on Mom. Every night, when me, Joe, and Larry would leave our house to go hang out in MBS schoolyard, I could see the worry on Mom's face. She knew we stood a good chance of getting hurt in a fight, or worse. And she had no way of knowing what was going on while we were out. Like so many other parents in our neighborhood, she'd just wait at home, hoping and praying. Hours later, when the three of us returned home, Mom's face would light up with a glow of relief.

I'm sure Mom would have preferred that we didn't go out. But she knew we were at an age when we had to go out and be with our friends. Some white parents in the neighborhood refused to let their kids go out for any reason except to go to school. I'm sure some black parents were doing the same with their kids. I used to think how awful that must be, to be a 12-year-old who's not allowed out of his house. I'd much rather be out with our friends, taking our chances.

The situation in our neighborhood had gotten so bad that me, Joe, and Larry couldn't even go to the grocery store for Mom anymore without getting attacked. There were three corner grocery stores a short walk from our house. The one on 57th and Chester Avenue wouldn't let us run up a bill, so we never bought groceries there. The other two grocery stores were at 58th and Chester Avenue and 57th and Kingsessing Avenue.

Usually, we shopped at the grocery store at 58th and Chester Avenue, which was closest to our house. The store was owned by four brothers. They were all nice men who always let us buy groceries there and put it on our bill. Whenever I was buying groceries and it was time to pay, I'd just say, "Put it on our bill, please." Whichever brother was at the checkout counter would reach below and pull out a big cigar box. Inside the cigar box was a stack of long, thin pieces of white cash-register-tape paper. Each slip of paper had the name of a different family in big letters across the top. And each slip of paper had a list of IOUs written in ink below the family name. Our family's bill always seemed to have IOUs written on both sides of the paper.

That summer, our bill at the grocery store on 58th and Chester Avenue got so high they wouldn't let us put anything else on the bill until we paid some of it off. So we started shopping at the grocery store near 57th and Kingsessing Avenue. The man who owned that grocery store was also a nice man. He had no problem with us running up a bill. Unfortunately, shopping at his store became a problem for a different reason.

One day after school, when I went to buy groceries for Mom, a group of about seven black kids about my age were hanging out right across the street from the grocery store, in front of the shoemaker's store. I was hoping that this was just a one-day thing, that this wasn't going to be their new hangout. But I was wrong. That group of black kids started hanging out on that corner every day. So just about every time me, Joe, or Larry went to that grocery store, we had trouble. We'd either get into fights, get chased home, or both. I never liked grocery shopping in the first place. I always thought it was a pain in the butt. Now having to go grocery shopping felt like a combat mission. Many times, when I'd get close to 57th Street, I'd see the black kids hanging out that I knew were going to mess with me. So I'd turn around and go back home. I'd watch TV for about an hour. Then I'd try to go to the grocery store again, hoping the coast would be clear.

Other times when I did buy groceries there, the storeowner would walk up to Kingsessing Avenue with me and watch after me as I walked the half-block back to Cecil Street. If no customers were in his store, he would stand on the corner the entire time until he saw that I made it back to Cecil Street safely.

Mom couldn't go grocery shopping because she'd recently had some surgery and was supposed to be off her feet for a while. It was Mom's fifth surgery in the last few years. Whenever I asked Mom why she had to go to the hospital so often, she'd say it was "woman problems." She said giving birth to five boys in six-and-a-half years had taken its toll on her body. I always knew how tough Mom was, but I'd never seen more strength in any person than I did watching Mom recover from her surgeries. The doctor told her to stay off her feet for a few weeks. Yet, within a matter of days, Mom would be out of bed, hobbling around the house in obvious pain, with one hand always pressing against her lower stomach area. It seemed like no matter how much pain Mom was in, the only thought in her mind was that she had to take care of Dad and her five boys. It was never about her. It was always about us.

Even though Mom was able to hobble around the house, she was in no shape to go grocery shopping. And now that me, Joe, and Larry were getting attacked almost every time we tried to go shopping, we had a problem. Mom had to come up with another plan. So she began sending our two younger brothers to the store. Marty and Steven were nine and seven years old at the time. Mom figured that there was no way the black kids who were hanging out near the grocery store would mess with a nine- and seven-year-old.

For a couple weeks, Mom's strategy worked. But it wasn't long before the black kids, who knew Marty and Steven were our brothers, caught on that they were now going to the grocery store instead of us. One day, one of those black kids, a 13-year-old named Duane, chased Marty and Steven home from the store and warned them to never come back. That was the end of Marty and Steven's shopping days, and it made me want to get even with Duane more than ever before.

Duane was a punk. He was one of the first black kids to move into our neighborhood. Me and my brothers would walk past Duane's house on our way back and forth to school. When Duane first moved into our neighborhood, I remember seeing how well he was treated by all his white neighbors. They even used to throw birthday parties for him. I didn't have a problem with any of that. At the time, Duane seemed like a nice kid. We were about the same age, and we'd say "hi" whenever we passed each other on the street.

My problem with Duane started when more and more black kids began moving into the neighborhood. As Duane started hanging out with a bigger and bigger group, he liked to mess with us whenever his group outnumbered ours. So when Marty and Steven told me it was Duane who chased them home, I was more determined than ever to get even with him when the time was right.

I felt bad for Marty and Steven. When I was their age, I was having the time of my life, spending all day, every day, playing game after game with lots of kids my age in Myers playground. The only time Marty and Steven could go out of the house was when Mom or Dad walked them over to a friend's house. They couldn't even go out for Halloween.

Halloween for me, Joe, and Larry used to be so much fun. We'd each take two pillowcases, one stuffed inside the other. Then we'd go trick-or-treating up and down street after street of row homes. As soon as our first pillowcase was filled with candy, we'd pull out the second pillowcase. We knew we could fill the second one, too, if we wanted to. The supply of houses we could go to was endless. But we'd usually get tired when the second pillowcase was about halfway filled, and we'd head back home.

Now Halloween night was nothing like it used to be. The few people who took kids trick-or-treating would do it right after school, before dark. Used to be that we had to wait until *after* dark before we could even start trick-or-treating. Fortunately, Marty and Steven did get to wear their Halloween costumes to school for the day, and Mom would take them to a couple of stores and some neighbors' houses on their way home from school so they could get some candy.

Marty and Steven were pretty much confined to our house. Whenever they wanted to go outside to play, the only place they could play was out in front of our house. Before long, both of them became very good at step-ball, a game they could play right on our front steps. In step-ball, the object was to throw the air ball against the front steps, hoping the ball will hit the corner of one of the concrete steps and ricochet into the air. If the ball went over the public church fence across the street, it was a home run. If the ball hit the fence in the air, it was a triple. Every other ball that wasn't caught was a single. Marty and Steven played so much step-ball, I didn't even want to play them anymore. I knew there was a good chance they would beat me. And there was no way I wanted to lose to my younger brothers.

When Marty and Steven got tired of playing step-ball, they played basketball, using the telephone pole in front of our house as their basket. Over the years, me, Joe, and Larry played hundreds of games using that pole as our basket. Screwed into the pole about eight feet off the ground was an oval-shaped piece of metal, about six inches long, with a serial number etched into it. That piece of metal was our target. When the basketball hit the metal, it made a loud, clanging sound, which let everyone know the shot counted.

Youngest brother Steven in 1971, playing basketball in front of our house near the telephone pole we used as our basket. Presbyterian church property is in background.

When Marty and Steven got tired of playing basketball, they'd have a catch with a football in front of our house. One Saturday afternoon, even a simple football catch turned into an adventure. I remember I was sitting in the house watching the Phillies on TV when Steven walked into the house. He didn't look happy.

"Do we have another football?" he asked me.

"Dad just bought you guys a football," I said.

"I know," Steven said, "Me and Marty were having a catch with it. When the football hit the telephone pole, it bounced up the street. When it got near the alley, a black kid jumped out, grabbed the ball, and ran away with it."

It didn't seem fair that Marty and Steven had to experience this kind of stuff at an age when they should have been having the time of their lives, just enjoying being kids. But they never complained about it. It was the only life they knew. They had no idea what they were missing. And that was probably a good thing.

CHAPTER 13
August, 1971:
Father Walt's Reality Check

MOM DIDN'T HAVE any sisters. She had just one brother, Uncle Walt, who was a Catholic priest serving in Georgia. When Uncle Walt was a boy, he got polio during a time when polio was infecting lots of young kids. Fortunately, the doctors got Uncle Walt's polio under control before he became paralyzed like a lot of other kids. Uncle Walt did end up with some permanent damage to his left leg that forced him to walk with a noticeable limp.

Uncle Walt once told me that he knew he wanted to be a priest from the time he was in high school. Unfortunately, when he graduated from high school, he couldn't get into the seminary in the Philly area because of his polio-damaged leg. So he applied to a seminary in Maryland and was accepted. Because he went to a seminary in the South, the deal was that he had to serve in the South when he became a priest. At the time, Uncle Walt, or "Father Walt" as everyone else called him, was serving as pastor at a parish near Savannah, Georgia.

Every August, Uncle Walt would come north to spend his month of vacation with us, his only extended family. And every August, he'd notice that the situation in our neighborhood was getting worse and worse. But it didn't seem to concern him. Uncle Walt used to say our situation was "a blessing from God."

"You have an opportunity here," he said, "for two races of people to learn to live together in peace."

When we'd tell him stories about all the trouble that was going on, he'd just shrug it off, saying, "Just take it one day at a time. Be nice to each other. And everything will be fine."

I said, "Uncle Walt, that all sounds good. But it's not as easy as you think. It's crazy out there."

He still wasn't buying it. "Kevin," he said, "things can't be that bad."

I knew things could be worse. In fact, just a few days earlier, I heard about something that was a lot worse. I was sitting in the Vittle Vat's dining room eating lunch at a table right next to some of the older Dirty Annies. Evidently one of them was 18 years old. And he was scared.

"Man, if my birthday gets a low number," he said, "I'm goin' to Canada. I ain't getting my head shot off in Nam." He was talking about the Vietnam War Draft Lottery that was going to be on TV that night.

"You gonna watch?" one of the guys he was sitting with asked him.

"No way I'm watchin'," the 18-year-old kid answered, "I can't watch. With my luck, January 14th will be number one. My mom and dad are gonna watch and let me know what happens. They're more scared than I am."

After hearing that conversation, I decided to watch. That night, on live television, 366 plastic balls were randomly picked out of a rotating drum. It was like a big game of bingo, only the lives of 18-year-olds were at stake. Inside each ball was a date with a number assigned to it. That night, the date December 4th had the number "one" assigned to it. That meant 18-year-olds born on December 4th would be the first to be drafted into the Vietnam war. The kid from the Dirty Annies was lucky. His birthday, January 14th, was assigned number 285, which was so far down the list he might not even get called up.

If I were 18, I would have been petrified knowing those plastic balls in that drum could play a big role in how long I lived. In just the past three years, about 30,000 Americans had gotten killed fighting in Vietnam. I'd see video from the battlefield on TV every night when Dad would watch the news. And every night the man on the news would give the war's death count as if he were giving the Phillies score. It was as if he was saying, "Today, the Phillies lost four-to-three, and eight more kids were killed in Vietnam."

One night, one of those kids in the death count was our neighbor, Tommy Dugan. Tommy lived across the alley behind us on Alden Street. He was about seven or eight years older than me, about 19 or 20. Tommy lived next door to a kid that me and my two brothers used to hang out with when we were younger. We always used to sit on the front steps that were connected to Tommy's front steps. So we saw Tommy a lot. Tommy always found time to talk with us. A lot of guys his age wouldn't even say "hi" to kids our age. But Tommy went out of his way to spend some time with us. Many times, before Tommy would go out to meet up with his friends, he'd even find time to play a quick game of box-ball with us on Alden Street.

Tommy got shot in his hand. Word around the neighborhood was that he was going to be OK. Then his hand got some kind of infection, and they had to amputate one of his fingers. But the infection continued to spread, and Tommy died. I was so sad when I heard Tommy died. He was one of those older guys I really looked up to, the kind of guy I wanted to be like when I got older. But now the Vietnam war had taken his life.

I didn't know much about the Vietnam war. As I said, the only part of the *Bulletin* I usually read was the sports section. So all I knew about Vietnam was what I saw on TV. It seemed like we'd been fighting the Vietnam war my entire life. In my mind, the Vietnam war was like this big black hole that lots of kids went into and far too many never came out of. I prayed the war would end before me and my brothers got old enough to have to go. Lots of people wanted the war to end, especially young people. Seemed like almost every night on the news, they'd show anti-war protests from somewhere in the country. About a year earlier, one of those protests turned ugly. It happened during an anti-war protest at Kent State University in Ohio. Four unarmed college students got shot and killed by the Ohio National Guard who were trying to break up the anti-war protest. The newsman said that two of the students who were killed weren't even involved in the protest. They got shot just walking to class. The whole Vietnam war situation was scary just thinking about it. It made what was going on in our neighborhood seem like it wasn't so bad.

Still, our situation was bad, and Uncle Walt had no idea how bad. But his outlook changed real fast one hot and humid Tuesday afternoon when he got a first-hand look at just how dangerous our neighborhood had become.

When Uncle Walt came north every August, he stayed with our grandmother, who we called "Nonna." Nonna lived in a row home on Frazier Street, just a block and a half from our house and right up the street from MBS School. Nonna lived so close to MBS that we'd often eat lunch at her house instead of going all the way home for lunch. I loved watching TV at Nonna's house. She had the first TV I'd ever seen with a remote control. It was so cool to be able to change channels on the TV without having to get up off the sofa.

Uncle Walt looked forward to spending his vacation with us every August. And we were happy to see him. He was always nice to us. And he was very generous to us, despite how thrifty he was. Me and my brothers used to laugh at how Uncle Walt would use the same tea bag four or five times. One of his favorite sayings to us was, "Waste not, want not, young men."

Another reason we were so happy to have Uncle Walt around was because Uncle Walt had a car. Which meant, for one month every year, we had a car. Sometimes, on really hot days, Uncle Walt would take us to visit friends of his who had a swimming pool, which was a definite upgrade from getting wet under the fireplug on Cecil Street until the cops came and shut it off.

We never had a pool in our neighborhood. If we wanted to swim in a pool, we had to walk a couple miles to Finnegan playground near 70th Street and Woodland Avenue, where they had a built-in pool. Actually, we did have a pool at Myers playground for a short time. A couple summers before, the playground workers put up an above-ground pool shaped like a small ice-skating rink about 50 feet long. The day the pool opened, the weather was hot and sunny. There must have been at least a hundred kids squeezed shoulder-to-shoulder into that pool. No one had room to actually swim. The pool was way too crowded, and the water seemed to get dirtier by the minute. Younger kids were getting banged around by older kids who were wrestling in the jam-packed pool. The pool didn't stay up for long. After just a couple weeks, the playground workers took it down. So on really hot days, we were back under the fireplug on Cecil Street.

Every August, when Uncle Walt came north, he'd also take us down the shore for a couple day-trips. When Uncle Walt wasn't taking us places, Mom had him taking her places. Mom had a long list of places she wanted Uncle Walt to take her while he was here with his car. I'd always heard that it was Mom's long list of car trips that convinced Dad to quit driving. Mom never had a license, so she constantly had Dad drive her and Nonna all over the streets of Southwest and South Philly. But Dad put an end to that. The way I heard it: right after I was born, Dad simply didn't renew his license, sold his big black Chevy, and never drove again.

Years later, when I asked Dad about it, he said, "Kev, I could take the "13" trolley on Chester Avenue to work. I could walk to the grocery store.

I could walk to the bar. And I was tired of driving your mom and Nonna all over the city. What the hell did I need a car for?"

I laughed out loud when Dad told me that, although I heard Mom didn't find it funny at all when it happened. But it was so typical of Dad, always trying to make life simpler.

When Uncle Walt wasn't taking us on road trips, he'd be at our house a lot, hanging around and spending as much time as he could with us. On this particular Tuesday afternoon, Uncle Walt was in our house with Nonna and Mom as five of us were playing street-hockey out in front of our house. It was me, Joe, Larry, and the two Collins brothers, Terry and Mark, who loved to play street-hockey a lot more than I did. I'd much rather play box-ball or football on the street. But if everyone else wanted to play hockey, I was happy to join in.

Our hockey goal consisted of two, two-by-four pieces of wood about three feet long. We'd lay them flat on the street about six feet apart. They were easy to move out of the way every five minutes or so when a car would drive down our narrow, one-way street. Our hockey sticks had plastic blades, a new invention that saved us a lot of money. Whenever our more expensive, wooden hockey sticks would break, we'd take the trolley to a sporting goods store in Center City that sold plastic blades we could screw into the handle of our broken hockey sticks. Then we'd heat the blade over our stove's flame until the plastic was soft enough to bend into a left-handed or right-handed curve. Those plastic blades lasted a long time, and saved us from having to keep buying wooden hockey sticks that cost so much and broke so easily.

Because there were only five of us playing hockey that day, we played a game of two-against-two with Mark Collins as the designated goalie. Mark had old sofa cushions tied to his legs with neckties his father didn't wear anymore. And he was using my mom's wicker broom as his goalie stick.

We were right in the middle of our hockey game when I heard glass shattering near us. I looked up and saw about a dozen black kids charging toward us from Kingsessing Avenue. They were throwing bottles and running at us with broom handles and belts. We were outnumbered badly, so we all ran into our house. As soon as Mom and Uncle Walt went out onto our front porch to see what was happening, the black kids ran back up to Kingsessing Avenue. We knew who the kids were. It was Duane and his friends, the same guys who would mess with us whenever we tried to go to the grocery store near 57th and Kingsessing Avenue.

This was the first time Uncle Walt had ever seen anything like this.

I remember him saying, "I can't believe they'd bother you when you're playing right in front of your own house." He was shocked, but not nearly as shocked as he would be an hour later.

When things settled down, the Collins brothers decided to walk home. But Mom didn't want them walking home alone. She knew they'd have to walk right past the kids who'd just attacked us.

"No problem," Uncle Walt said, "I'll walk them home."

Uncle Walt didn't have his car with him that day. He and Nonna had walked together from Nonna's house to our house. Uncle Walt asked me to go with him. So me and Uncle Walt set off to walk the Collins brothers to their house on 57th Street, less than a block away from our house.

I figured that, even if the kids who attacked us were still hanging out, we'd be safe walking in broad daylight with Uncle Walt dressed in his priest uniform: black shoes, black pants, and black shirt with the white collar.

As soon as we got to Kingsessing Avenue, I saw that the guys who had attacked us were hanging out on the other side of Kingsessing Avenue, near Alden Street. Uncle Walt saw them, too. He kept telling us in a soft whisper that everything would be alright. "Just keep walking," he said, "and look straight ahead. Just keep looking straight ahead."

I couldn't help but sneak a quick glance across the street. That's when I noticed two of the bigger guys from the group walking across Kingsessing Avenue directly toward us. One had a broom handle in his right hand. I was concerned, but I was still convinced there was no way they'd mess with us while we were walking with a priest in broad daylight.

As the two guys got closer and closer, Uncle Walt kept saying, "Don't worry. Look straight ahead and keep walking. God will protect us."

So that's what we did, until I heard the "WHACK!" of the broom handle cracking against Terry Collins' forehead. Blood gushed out from the cut on his head and spilled down the right side of his face.

"Hey, hey," Uncle Walt shouted, "why'd you do that, young man?"

The two guys ran back across Kingsessing Avenue to join their friends who were pointing and laughing at Terry, now doubled over in pain, pulling the bottom of his tee shirt to his head to try to stop the bleeding. In less than a minute, a cop car that had been circling the area sped over to where the four of us were standing. The black kids took off running down Alden Street toward Greenway Avenue.

The cop gave Terry a towel to press against the cut. I showed the cop where Terry lived, pointing to his house less than a half-block away. The cop then drove Terry and his brother Mark to their house. Me and Uncle Walt followed them on foot. When Mrs. Collins came out and saw Terry bleeding the way he was, she began crying hysterically as Uncle Walt tried to explain what had happened. Because Mrs. Collins' husband had the family car at work, Mrs. Collins ran back into her house to get her pocketbook so she and her son Mark could ride with the cop to get Terry to the hospital.

When Mrs. Collins ran back into her house, Uncle Walt walked over to the cop, who was black, and said, "Officer, I had no idea how dangerous this neighborhood has become."

I didn't say anything, but I thought to myself, What do you think I've been tryin' to tell you?

The cop looked at Uncle Walt and said, "Reverend, it's gettin' more and more dangerous around here by the day."

When the cop car left for the hospital, me and Uncle Walt began our walk home. I was nervous. My eyes were scanning back and forth to see if those guys were still around. I knew now that even walking with a priest in broad daylight wouldn't keep us safe. Fortunately, the black kids were nowhere in sight.

When we got home, we told Mom and my brothers what happened. Mom was really upset. I tried to calm her down, saying, "Mom, Terry's at the hospital now with his mom. There's nothing we can do."

She eventually calmed down a little. But Uncle Walt remained in a state of shock. About three hours later, Mom called Mrs. Collins. Terry needed eight stitches to close the cut.

Later that night, after we ate dinner, I heard Uncle Walt tell Mom that she'd better think seriously about moving us out of the neighborhood. Mom agreed. She told Uncle Walt that she and Dad had already talked about moving the day Marty and Steven got chased home from the grocery store. But after what happened to Terry that day, Mom decided to take action.

"I'm calling the realtor tomorrow," I heard Mom say to Uncle Walt.

I still didn't want to move. I still loved living in our neighborhood. Even though a lot of friends had already moved out, a lot of friends still lived here. And despite all the trouble around us, we still had a great time together. Besides, summer was almost over, so a lot of my friends would soon be coming back from the shore. One other reason I definitely didn't want to move was because I was headed into eighth grade, and I was looking forward to my last year playing football and basketball for MBS.

CHAPTER 14
September, 1971:
Our Almost-Safe Haven

OVER THE YEARS, I learned that there were only two ways to get respect on the streets in our neighborhood. I either had to be one of the tough guys, or I had to be good in sports. I was definitely *not* one of the tough guys. Our neighborhood was full of guys a whole lot tougher than me. Fortunately, like all my brothers, I was pretty good in sports. And if I stayed healthy, there was a good chance I'd be in the starting line-up for my last season on the MBS football and basketball teams.

Even with all the racial trouble at Myers playground, our football team continued to practice in the playground every weeknight in the fall. We were still safe there. We had seven adult coaches. Our head coach was the Supervisor at Myers playground. So he knew nearly everybody, white and black, who came into the playground. Of course, another one of our coaches was Officer Tom McGlone. Tom always had a gun tucked away on one hip, and handcuffs tucked away on the other. Even though Tom was an undercover cop, I had a feeling the black kids who liked to start trouble knew who Tom was. I knew for a fact that the white kids who liked to start trouble knew who Tom was.

My favorite football coach was a young guy in his twenties who coached our offense. Everyone called him Buddy. Buddy played for West Catholic's football team in the mid-sixties. He had a great sense of humor that kept the team loose. Plus, he was a smart coach, always coming up with new plays that seemed to confuse the defense. Buddy was one of those coaches who became more than just a football coach to me. I developed a close relationship with him, close enough that I could talk to him about girlfriend problems, and personal stuff like that. Having Buddy as a coach was like having a second father at football practice every night.

Because football practice was only a half-block from our house, we didn't have any trouble walking back and forth to practice. But many of the kids on our team who lived four or five blocks away from Myers playground did have trouble. I heard a lot of stories about kids on our team, black and white, getting into fights and getting chased on their way home from football practice.

MBS football was a big deal in our neighborhood. Just about every young boy wanted to play football for MBS when he got older. Lots of parents, neighbors, and older guys from the neighborhood came to all our home games. The games were on Saturday mornings at Myers playground, usually at 10 o'clock. Sometimes the crowd along our sideline was two or three rows deep. Our biggest game every year was our Thanksgiving Day rivalry against St. Barnabas. The week leading up to our Thanksgiving game was one of my favorite weeks of the year.

On Monday of Thanksgiving week, every player on our team got a hat with the letters "MBS" stenciled on it. Every year, the hat was a different style: from berets to cowboy hats to knitted hats. All the players on the football team were allowed to wear their hats during school the entire week. I could tell some of the stricter nuns were not happy about us wearing our hats in class. But they couldn't do anything to stop it. It had become an MBS tradition.

On Wednesday afternoon of Thanksgiving week, students and parents packed MBS gym for a pep rally. Later that night, the coaches lit a big bonfire at Myers playground.

Early Thanksgiving morning, the team and the coaches gathered for Mass at MBS Church. We went to Mass as a team the morning before every football game. If we didn't go to Mass, we didn't play in the game. After Mass on Thanksgiving morning, we'd walk over to MBS gym for a special team breakfast.

After breakfast, when the team got back together at Myers playground, we got our first look at our new helmets. They weren't actually new. They were newly painted. Every year, during the week leading up to the Thanksgiving-Day game, our coaches and some parents got together and painted all 50 helmets with a different design, giving the team a fresh new look for our big game. We never knew what our helmets would look like until a couple hours before the game. It was so exciting. What made it even more exciting was that we played the Thanksgiving game at Bartram High's field, which meant I got to play on the same field West Catholic played on.

Team photo of MBS 1971-72 football team at Myers playground.

As the football season got under way, it looked like we might have a pretty good team. My brother Larry was one of the only seventh graders who started. Me and Larry were the starting safeties on defense. Larry was very athletic with long arms that helped him break up and intercept a lot of passes. I was really proud that, even as a seventh-grader, Larry was such a big part of our team. Plus, all my eighth-grade friends loved having Larry on the field with us. And I do mean *all* my eighth-grade friends. Everyone we hung out with was on the team, including two of my best friends, Chris and Donny.

Chris was about five-foot-seven, an inch or so shorter than me. But he was fearless on the football field. He loved to dive horizontally into tackles with little regard for his body. I always called him "the best 125-pound linebacker I ever saw." Chris was fun to be around. No matter where we were, no matter what we were doing, Chris was just happy to be there, hanging out with the boys.

As upbeat as Chris always was, Donny took upbeat to an even higher level. Donny was the happiest guy I ever met, always smiling and singing whatever songs were popular on the radio. We'd be walking down Kingsessing

Avenue and Donny would pretend he was Tony Orlando, singing the song "Knock Three Times" into his invisible microphone at the top of his lungs. And the best part about Donny was that he didn't care who heard him singing. He was just having fun being Donny.

Donny was also the most polite kid in our crowd. All our parents loved Donny. Every time he'd come over to our house, he'd say something like, "Hey Mrs. Purcell, how ya feeling today? You look especially nice. I love your hair." He was a natural charmer. It wasn't surprising so many girls our age liked Donny, too.

On the football field, Donny was an absolute terror. He was a good inch taller than me, very strong, and definitely one of the best players on our team. Donny played cornerback on defense. I was a running back on offense. A lot of times at practice, I'd have to run the ball to Donny's side of the field. Before the ball was snapped, I'd sneak a quick glance in Donny's direction. He'd be at his cornerback position, singing out loud and playing his invisible guitar as he waited for the play to start. He looked harmless. But I knew as soon as I crossed the line of scrimmage with the ball, he'd turn into a wild animal ready to rip my head off.

We went to all our road football games in a rented bus that was green and white with rounded corners, just like the "G" bus that traveled up and down 58th Street. Each player on the team had to chip in three dollars to rent the bus. It was worth every penny. Those bus rides were so much fun. On the way to the games, we'd get all fired-up, singing MBS fight songs and banging on the sides of the bus as we travelled through the city streets. If we won the game, the bus rides home were even more fun. We'd all start singing the jingle, "Everybody goes to Gino's," knowing there was a real good chance our coaches would tell the bus driver to pull over at the next Gino's hamburger joint we'd pass on our ride home. Then the coaches would chip in to buy all 50 of us a cheeseburger and a soda.

Of the 50 kids on MBS' football team that year, 10 were black, the most black kids that, up to that time, had ever played on any MBS team. Because we had so many black kids on our team, we'd sometimes run into trouble on road games in white neighborhoods. One Saturday, we'd just beaten an all-white team in an all-white neighborhood down in South Philly. Just as our team bus began to pull away from the field, we were bombarded with rocks by a gang of white kids yelling racial stuff at the black kids on our team. Our coaches immediately yelled for everyone to put their helmets back on. Two bus windows were shattered, but nobody got hurt. It was scary. But, in a way, it was kind of ironic, too. I got to thinking that here we were under attack by a white gang. If me and Larry were to get messed with by black kids on our walk home later, we'd be attacked by both a white gang and a black gang on the same day. Fortunately, that didn't happen. Me and Larry didn't have any problems on our walk home that day.

For the most part, everybody on our football team got along. That's not to say there weren't some tense moments. There were a couple kids on the team, white and black, who would carry the racial stuff onto the practice field with an occasional late hit or some other dirty play. Those cheap shots weren't tolerated by our coaches. Whoever was out of line was reamed out in front of the team and forced to run long laps around the playground for punishment. Overall, we were a close-knit team of black and white kids working together to try to win football games for MBS. And we won our share. We finished the season with eight wins and three losses. Unfortunately, one of those losses was against St. Barnabas on Thanksgiving Day.

Playing sports was like therapy to me. At a time when nothing else going on around me seemed to make any sense anymore, sports still made sense. It forced us to put all the racial stuff aside and work together for a common goal. Other than sports, I can't think of any other set of circumstances that would have brought white kids and black kids together the way sports brought us together.

In school, writing was my escape. Whenever I was writing, I was at peace. All the trouble going on around the neighborhood temporarily disappeared from my mind. And I usually got good grades on my writing assignments. One day, my English teacher asked me to join the school newspaper staff. I joined, and I liked it a lot. Putting a newspaper together was like putting a big puzzle together with a clock ticking. I enjoyed the excitement and the pressure. But working on the newspaper led to another problem. Because we did all of our newspaper work after school, we all walked home at different times. That meant I often had to walk home from MBS alone, instead of with the group that walked home together right after school when a cop car was still parked on every corner.

By the time I'd leave MBS, it was usually around 4:30, giving me just enough time to get home, get something to eat, and get ready for football practice at six. By that time, the cop cars had already left their posts, and black kids were usually hanging out on both Kingsessing Avenue and Chester Avenue, my only possible routes home. Most times I didn't even know which route I'd take until I scouted things out. The nicer the weather, the more careful I had to be. I never turned a corner until I took a peek around it. Then, depending on what I'd see, I'd sneak in and out of alleys to get past the areas where the black kids were hanging out. As soon as I was in the clear, I'd run as fast as I could the rest of the way home. Somehow, I always managed to get home safely. I was usually out of breath, but I was safe.

Shortly after football season ended, basketball season started right up. We practiced in MBS gym every weeknight, and we played our games at MBS gym every weekend. We had a pretty good basketball team, too. Me, Larry, Chris, and Donny were all on the team. We won the tough Southwest Philly division, but we lost in the quarter-finals of the city tournament.

That winter, I was so busy with basketball, the school newspaper, and homework that I didn't have a lot of free time. So I hardly ever made it over to Myers gym. Which meant I didn't see all the changes that were happening over there. But I heard about them. For most of the fall and into the holidays, the indoor gym at Myers was still being used by white kids, including a lot of the Dirty Annies who played basketball there almost every night. The black guys still wouldn't go into the gym. Then, one night after the holidays, it all changed.

The way I heard it, the night started out as a normal night at the gym. Lots of white kids, including a lot of the Dirty Annies, were hanging out and playing pick-up basketball. All of a sudden, about eight black kids from 58th and Greenway Avenue, the same kids who were always fighting with the Dirty Annies, walked into Myers gym and went right up to the basketball court. Two playground workers who saw what was happening sensed there might be trouble. They stood on the sideline at half-court to keep an eye on things.

The biggest black kid, a defensive tackle on the football team at Bartram High, yelled, "We got winners" loud enough for the kids who were playing to hear. Because nobody else had already called "winners," the black kids had the right to play the winners of the game in progress.

When the game started, I heard things got rough in a hurry. Both teams were fouling each other so hard it wasn't long before a full-scale brawl broke out on the basketball court. The playground workers rushed onto the court with arms extended, trying to separate the two groups. But they couldn't stop the fight. Within minutes, cops rushed into the gym to get things under control. From that night on, there was always at least one cop stationed inside Myers gym. Now that there was always a cop in the gym, the black kids finally felt safe enough to hang out there. And before long, so many black kids were hanging in Myers gym that it was now the white kids who never went into the gym anymore. I never set foot in Myers gym again.

When Father McMurtry and our coaches from MBS found out that it wasn't safe for us to hang out in Myers gym anymore, they decided to open MBS gym for us on weeknights to give us a place to hang out. So that's where we went every night to get out of the cold, have some fun, and play some basketball. We had a great time every night, until it was time for everyone to walk home our separate ways. That's when things got dangerous.

CHAPTER 15
March, 1972:
Murder on 59th Street

THE WEATHER WAS way too warm for the first day of March. While we were in school, the temperature had climbed into the seventies. Once I got home, I did my homework, had a quick dinner, and got ready to go over to MBS gym with my two brothers to hang out and play basketball.

I took the usual safety precautions. I wore my belt with the thick buckle. On the way out, I grabbed my car antenna from its hideout in our front garden and slid it up the sleeve of my spring coat. I couldn't believe I was actually wearing my spring coat. Just the day before, I was wearing my heavy, green Army jacket. But this was one of those unusually warm, winter days when everybody who'd been cooped up indoors for weeks was so excited to finally be outdoors again. Because so many people were outdoors, I had a feeling it could be a dangerous night. I admit the warm air felt great, but I still wished the weather was bitter cold, so fewer kids, if any, would be hanging out on the corners.

When me, Joe, and Larry got to the bottom of Cecil Street, I peeked around the corner to see who was hanging out on Chester Avenue. I didn't like what I saw. Eight black guys, including two guys we called "Big Rob" and "Red Sneakers," were hanging out in front of the Vittle Vat sandwich shop. Both Big Rob and Red Sneakers were new to the area, and they both liked to mess with us all the time. We gave Big Rob his nickname because he was about six-foot-three, strong, and a really tough fighter. Every time I saw his face, I knew trouble was coming. Red Sneakers was about five-foot-10, quick, and sneaky. We called him Red Sneakers because he always wore bright red Converse All Stars. Converse had just started selling Converse All Stars in colors other than the usual black and white. Not too many kids wore the new colors when they first came out. Red Sneakers was one of the first, so his red Converse All Stars were easy to spot in a crowd.

Me and my brothers knew there was no way we'd make it past Big Rob, Red Sneakers, and their friends without getting into a fight. So the three of us quietly cut through the alley over to Alden Street, just past where the black kids were hanging out. Then we sprinted the rest of the way down Chester Avenue and into MBS schoolyard. When the black kids saw us, we could hear them yelling stuff at us. But we made it to the schoolyard, and we were safe for now. The problem was, because they saw us, they knew we'd be coming back later. And with the weather being so warm, I was pretty sure they'd be waiting for us on our way back home. But we could deal with that later. It was time to have fun.

Once inside MBS gym, we played pick-up basketball all night. The guys who weren't playing sat around talking about sports, girls, and school, usually in that order. We had a lot of fun. And it wasn't just white kids who came to MBS gym to play basketball. A few black kids from MBS parish usually played with us, including a tall, lanky kid who was the best player in the gym every night he showed up. I'd never seen the kid before. Once MBS started opening up the gym for us, he started showing up. I heard he lived up near 58th and Willows Avenue. The kid's name was Michael Brooks. He had long arms and legs that the rest of his body hadn't yet grown into. He had a quick first step, which was unusual for a lanky kid like him. And Michael could snake his way through the smallest of openings and somehow end up at the basket. Plus, he could hit the outside jump shot. I loved playing on Michael's team because I knew there was a great chance we'd stay on the floor to play the guys who had "winners."

MBS gym usually closed around nine o'clock. Then came the hard part, getting home safe. And that night, as warm as it was, getting home safe figured to be even more difficult. We knew we could easily run into trouble on either Kingsessing Avenue or Chester Avenue.

At least there were eight of us starting out together. Our friend Chris lived in the other direction, near 57th and Woodland Avenue. He often had to walk home alone. Lots of times he'd tell us how he'd have to run, hunched over, using parked cars for cover as he scanned the area looking for the safest way to make his break past the black kids who hung out near his house.

Even though eight of us were walking together that night, we still had to be careful. We decided Chester Avenue would be our safest route home, despite the fact that Big Rob, Red Sneakers, and friends had been hanging out on Chester Avenue just a few hours earlier. Chester Avenue was usually our safest route. Kingsessing Avenue was darker and didn't have as many stores along the way. Chester Avenue was well lit with seven or eight stores lining our walk home, including Dirty Annie's, the Vittle Vat, and Cahill's Tavern.

Mom and Dad always told us that if we were ever in trouble on Chester Avenue, we should run into Cahill's. The bar was usually crowded. Lots of men from the neighborhood would stop there after work for some drinks. Plus, Cahill's sponsored a lot of bar-league sports teams, so the guys on the teams would come back to the bar for some drinks after each game. All the men who drank in Cahill's were white. Once in a while, black guys would stop in for takeout beer, but they rarely, if ever, stayed and had a drink at the bar.

One time, about a year earlier, I did run into Cahill's when I was in trouble. Four black kids tried to jump me one night as I was walking out of Dirty Annie's after buying some peanut butter Tastykakes. I was able to get away, so I ran across Chester Avenue and, for the first time in my life, I went into Cahill's through the front door by myself. Kids and women were supposed to use the ladies' entrance on the side of the bar. But this was an emergency.

Dad wasn't bartending that night. As soon as I ran into the bar, the first guys I saw were Jeff and Sean, who were standing near the end of the bar, just a few feet from the front door. Because I was in Cahill's so many times visiting Dad, I knew most of the men who hung out in the bar, including Jeff and Sean. As soon as they saw me, I must have looked really scared. They both rushed over to my side.

"Kevin, what's wrong?" asked Jeff. Both Jeff and Sean were in their mid-twenties.

"Four black kids tried to jump me, but I was able to get away," I said as I tried to catch my breath.

"They still out there?" asked Jeff.

I looked out the bar's front window and the kids were still there, directly across the street, standing in front of Dirty Annie's store.

"Yeah, that's them," I said.

"Don't worry, Kev," said Sean, "we'll walk you home."

I got to know Jeff and Sean pretty well last New Year's Day, when me and my two brothers marched with them in Philly's Mummers Parade. For years, Cahill's had a comic club that performed a skit in the Mummers Parade every New Year's Day. And every year, it was a different skit. Last year, their skit was called "Finnegan's Wake," about an Irish guy in a coffin who suddenly comes back to life. When they decided to include three altar boys in their skit, they asked Dad if me, Joe, and Larry would be interested. We were excited to be a part of it. We didn't even have to make a costume. Because me, Joe, and Larry were already altar boys at MBS, we just wore our altar-boy robes, and sprayed gold paint over an old pair of shoes. Wearing gold shoes was a Mummers Parade tradition.

Cahill's skit won 3rd prize in their category that year. We might have finished even higher if about 20 empty beer cans hadn't fallen out the side door of our lead car. It happened at the worst possible time, just as we were passing the judges' stand at City Hall. Evidently, the last guy who threw an empty beer can into the car's back seat didn't shut the door all the way. As soon as the car made a turn, the door flew open, and all the empty beer cans spilled out onto Broad Street for all the judges and spectators to see. I'm sure that cost us a few points.

When Jeff and Sean walked out of Cahill's with me, the black kids immediately began walking the other way, toward 57th Street. Jeff, who seemed like he already had quite a few beers in him, yelled over to them, "You guys get the fuck out of here. And don't ever mess with my man Kevin again."

Then Jeff and Sean walked me to the bottom of Cecil Street, where they waited until they could see that I'd made it home safe.

Now, where was I? Oh yeah … so on this unusually warm March night, eight of us were heading out of MBS schoolyard toward Chester Avenue for our walk home after playing basketball. When we got to Alden Street, two of our friends left our group and headed up to their homes. Now there were just six of us. It was me, my brothers Joe and Larry, plus our friends John, Doug, and Tommy. John's our friend who was up in the tree with me and Joe during the Bartram protest march. John lived on Chester Avenue between 58th Street and 59th Street. Doug and Tommy lived near 60th Street, at the far end of MBS parish.

Doug was a quiet, reserved kid who was always smiling and never had a bad word to say about anybody. He was 15, a sophomore at West Catholic. After school, Doug worked at a beer distributor near his home. So we didn't see Doug much except when he'd come over to MBS at nights to play basketball. Doug wasn't a great basketball player, but he loved to play, and he always played hard. Plus, he was an unselfish player, the kind of kid everyone liked to have on their team to play tough defense and get some rebounds.

Like Doug, Tommy was also a quiet kid and a nice kid. And, like Doug, Tommy was also a sophomore at West Catholic. It wasn't surprising that Tommy and Doug were such good friends, especially considering that they lived so close to each other. On the basketball court, Tommy was really quick. I hated when he'd cover me on defense. He was so quick that he'd be right up on my stomach, never giving me any room to drive to the basket. And I definitely needed room to drive. I never became as good an outside shooter as my dad.

As the six of us continued our walk home along Chester Avenue, I was surprised at how quiet things were for such a warm night. Myers gym usually closed around the same time that MBS gym closed. Often, when both gyms closed at the same time, a group of black kids would be walking in one direction on Chester Avenue at the same time our group was walking in the other direction, heading right for each other. And there were usually a lot more of them than there were of us. Fortunately, the cops knew there could be trouble at that time of night when both gyms closed. So a cop car or two was usually cruising up and down Chester Avenue.

But on this warm night, as we got close to Cecil Street, nobody was around: no Dirty Annies, no black kids, no cops. Something didn't feel right. Suddenly, at least a dozen black guys jumped out from behind five or six cars parked directly across Chester Avenue from where we were walking. They were coming after us, and they were coming fast.

Because we were already past Cahill's, the six of us took off up Cecil Street, sprinting the 50 yards to our house as fast as we could. The black guys were right behind us. We made it into our house just in time. We were able to get inside and lock the front door just as the first black guy set foot on our front porch.

Usually, in the past, whenever we were being chased, the kids who were chasing us would go away once we ran into somebody's house. This group didn't go away. All of them came right up onto our small front porch and tried to force open the locked door.

Dad was bartending at Cahill's that night. So Mom was home alone with my two youngest brothers. When we ran into our house and locked the door, Mom ran out from the kitchen. She was angry. Mom didn't take any shit from anybody. I'm pretty sure my brother Joe inherited that trait from Mom. Even though all the black kids were still out on our front porch, Mom unlocked the front door and opened the storm door just wide enough to yell, "Get the hell out of here."

As soon as those words left her mouth, I saw a fist burst through the slightly opened storm door and make contact with the right side of Mom's face. Thank God the kid's fist also hit part of the storm door, breaking the impact of the punch just enough so that Mom wasn't seriously hurt. She was sore, but not nearly as sore as she would have been had the punch landed squarely. We got Mom out of the way, and the six of us kept pushing and pushing at the door until we finally got it shut and locked again.

I'd never felt such a terrible combination of anger and helplessness. Someone had just punched my mom in the face in our own house, and there was nothing I could do about it. The black kids on the porch were still trying to force their way in. If we had a gun in our house, I would have begun shooting out onto our front porch until I was out of bullets. As soon as the black kids heard police sirens getting closer, they took off running. The cops came to our house, wrote down information for their report, and drove John, Doug, and Tommy home.

The night Mom got hit in the face was a night I'll never forget. But it wasn't the worst thing that happened on our dangerous walks home after playing basketball at MBS. It wasn't even close.

A few weeks later, when MBS gym closed at the same time Myers gym closed, six of us were headed home from MBS by way of Chester Avenue. Again, it was me, Joe, Larry, John, Doug, and Tommy. I remember looking ahead and seeing a group of about 15 black guys a block ahead of us, walking directly toward us.

My eyes immediately shifted to the traffic on Chester Avenue. I was praying I'd see a shiny blue cop car. And there it was, slowly cruising down the avenue, keeping pace with the black guys who were walking toward us. As our two groups passed each other near Alden Street, the cop car came to a complete stop. Both cops in the car were staring us down, their stares daring anyone in either group to start any trouble. Neither group gave up any ground as shoulders banged shoulders. But that was it. Both our groups continued on their way.

As usual, our group thinned out along the route home. When me and my two brothers left our group at Cecil Street, only John, Doug, and Tommy remained. John would leave the group when they reached his house a block away. Then Doug and Tommy would continue on to the 60th Street area where they both lived.

About 10 minutes after me and my brothers got home, I remember hearing a lot of police sirens nearby. But I didn't give it a second thought. Police sirens usually howled all hours of the night.

The next morning I heard the phone ringing in my parents' bedroom unusually early, before we'd even gotten out of bed to get ready for school. Because me and Joe's bedroom was right next to Mom and Dad's room, I could easily hear Mom answer the phone.

Then I heard Mom scream like I never heard her scream before. "No! No! No!" she yelled. Something was definitely wrong.

I jumped down from my top bunk and ran into my parents' room. Mom was wiping tears from her eyes. After she got herself under control, Mom gathered the three of us older guys away from our younger brothers and told us what had happened. When Doug and Tommy continued walking home the previous night, they only made it as far as 59th Street. At 59th and Trinity Street, they where attacked by four black kids. Doug was stabbed to death.

The next day's *Evening Bulletin* said that four black youths approached Doug and Tommy and asked them for a dime. When Tommy said he didn't have any money, one of the black kids punched him in the face. At the same time, the *Bulletin* reported, another black kid pulled out a knife and stabbed Doug in the chest, killing him. The article also played up the fact that Doug was killed less than two blocks away from Police Commissioner O'Neil's house, which was over by 61st Street, an area that was still mostly white.

When Mom told us that Doug was dead, I put up an emotional shield. I heard what she said. I knew what it meant. But I refused to let it sink in. I was in total denial. There was no way a 15-year-old friend I was walking home with last night could be dead this morning. It just wasn't possible. I don't think I cried. I was too numb to cry.

The four black kids were arrested shortly after the murder when they were spotted running into a house near 59th and Chester Avenue. Three of them were later convicted of first-degree murder and sentenced to life in prison. I'm not sure what punishment the fourth kid got.

Of all the things that happened in this crazy neighborhood, Doug's death was, by far, the hardest to accept. I still haven't come to terms with it. I still feel like it was just a dream.

Four Accused Of Killing Boy Over a Dime

Victim, 15, Stabbed 2 Blocks From Home In Southwest Phila.

Four teen-agers were arrested today on charges of stabbing to death a 15-year-old Southwest Philadelphia boy who, with his companion, refused to give them a dime.

Philadelphia Evening Bulletin, *Newspaper clipping collection.*
Philadelphia, Temple University Libraries, Urban Archives.

View from Myers playground of 59th and Chester Avenue, the area where Doug got killed. Photo courtesy of Bill Dorsch.

What made Doug's death even harder to accept was this: Doug and Tommy never hung out with us on weekends, or were part of our so-called "gang." Doug worked a lot of hours at the beer distributor. I think Tommy had a job, too. They were just two nice kids who loved to play basketball with the boys in MBS gym. Nobody deserved to die that way. But Doug was probably the least deserving of all. And I never saw Tommy again after the night Doug was killed. No one did. I heard his family moved him out of the neighborhood the very next day. In fact, after Doug's death, there were four or five white kids from the neighborhood I never saw again. I heard they were all sent out of the neighborhood by their parents to live with relatives and to go to school in safer neighborhoods.

At MBS the day after Doug was killed, a group of social workers had already been rounded up to help us deal with Doug's death. I remember staring at one of them as he was standing in front of our class talking to us. I didn't hear a word he said. I just kept thinking to myself, There's nothing you or anyone else can say that can make any sense out of any of this shit.

My thoughts ranged from seeking revenge to a desire to get the hell out of this neighborhood. My anger grew deeper on the night of Doug's viewing. His viewing was at a popular funeral home near 53rd and Chester Avenue. Nearly all the families living in that area now were black. Dozens of us lined the sidewalk outside the funeral home as we waited to say our final goodbyes. There were lots of cops stationed outside the funeral home. There was even a TV cameraman, the first time I'd seen a TV cameraman in the neighborhood since the Bartram protest march. All of a sudden, we heard the voices of a group of black kids from a half-block away. They were laughing and yelling at us.

One yelled, "Y'all goin' to see the dead honky!"

A couple others kept chanting, "Dead honky! Dead honky!"

A bunch of us tried to go after them, but the cops held us back as the black kids scattered.

After Doug's death, Mom and Dad were more determined than ever to move us out of the neighborhood. But they still couldn't sell our house. And if they couldn't sell our house, we couldn't move. It was that simple. In the seven months our house had been up for sale, no one had come to look at it. Mom was so frustrated. To make matters even worse, Mom told me the realtor gave her some bad news. The realtor told Mom that, even if he found a buyer, our house was now only worth about $3,500. Mom was hoping she could get $6,000, which was still less than the $7,000 Mom and Dad paid for the house back in 1956. Looks like the realtors were right a few years earlier when they kept calling Mom, warning her that if she didn't sell her house soon, she wouldn't get much money for it later.

At least we didn't have the added pressure of having to sell to whites. We already had four black families living on Cecil Street. No white family wanted to be the first on their street to sell to a black family. Once word got out that a white family was the first to sell to blacks, most of the neighbors on the street got pretty upset.

A couple years earlier, the parents of one of my friends, a kid named Vinnie, were the first to sell to blacks on their street. Vinnie took a lot of heat for it. I remember we were still hanging out in Myers playground at the time. When Vinnie came walking into the playground to hang out with us, one of the guys said, "Here comes Vinnie. I just heard his parents broke their block."

As Vinnie got closer to our group, the taunting began.

"Hey, Vinnie, I heard your parents sold your house to niggers."

"So what? Everybody's doin' it," Vinnie shot back.

"Yeah, but your parents broke the block. That ain't cool."

"Hey, man, I'm sorry. I had nothing to do with it," Vinnie said. "Somebody was gonna break the block sooner or later."

Nowadays, selling to blacks was no big deal. Every block in the neighborhood already had at least one black family living there. Besides, no white families wanted to move into our area anymore. With all the trouble in our neighborhood all over the news, hardly any families, white or black, wanted to move into our area. And the few people who did want to move into our neighborhood had a slew of houses for sale to choose from. What were the chances they'd want to buy our tiny house?

Even though I knew my parents desperately wanted to move, I had no idea how they were going to do it if they couldn't sell our house. And I was pretty sure they had no idea, either. Mom was even working now, cleaning other people's houses two or three days a week. But the extra money Mom made went to help pay day-to-day bills. It wasn't going to help us move. I simply had to accept the fact that this was our life now. And it didn't look like it was going to get any better any time soon. If anything, it would probably get worse.

CHAPTER 16
June, 1972:
Escape to the Poconos

THE SUMMER AFTER Doug's murder, more of my friends than ever were headed down the shore. I wished I could've gone with them. Because so many of them would be gone, we didn't even think about hanging out at Myers playground that summer. So, for the second summer in a row, we hung out at MBS schoolyard.

But the situation at MBS schoolyard was also getting worse. We were more outnumbered than ever by black kids on every side of the school property. Fortunately, we were also surrounded by a lot of cops. They were literally everywhere, in cop cars and walking the beat. In fact, it was around this time that the city even added cops on horses to patrol the streets in our area. I never realized how big those horses were until the first time I stood right next to one. The cops riding the horses were so high off the ground we could see them from blocks away.

Hanging out in MBS schoolyard that summer was still a lot of fun, especially early in the night. We'd sit around playing cards, smoking cigarettes, talking, laughing, and having a good time together. The fights usually didn't start until after dark. One particular night was especially frightening.

That night, I think there were seven of us hanging out on the steps of the annex building in the schoolyard. Just after dark, about 10 black kids suddenly came charging toward us through the schoolyard entrance closest to Kingsessing Avenue. As soon as we heard them, we jumped up to see how many kids there were, and to figure out our next move. Then something really scary happened. The black guy leading the charge suddenly stopped about 20 yards from us, dropped down to one knee, and, with his hands together, pointed a shiny metal object at us. I couldn't tell if it was a gun or not. If it wasn't a gun, he definitely wanted us to think it was.

Donny yelled, "Gun. He's got a gun!"

All of us took off running out of the schoolyard toward Chester Avenue. I tried to run in a zigzag to throw off the shooter's aim in case he was targeting me. But no shots were fired. When a cop on horseback on Chester Avenue saw us running, his horse trotted toward us.

"What's goin' on?" asked the cop, looking down from high up on his horse.

"One of the black kids got a gun," Donny shouted as he pointed back into the schoolyard.

The cop immediately turned the horse in the direction of the schoolyard and the horse broke into a gallop, racing into the schoolyard toward Kingsessing Avenue, looking for the kid with the gun. I don't know if the cop ever caught him or not.

This gun stuff was starting to make me nervous. If we got hit with a bottle, a broom handle, or a car antenna, sure it would hurt. But it wasn't likely to kill us. How were we supposed to protect ourselves against guns? It looked like it was going to be another long, dangerous summer.

I was lucky that a couple really cool things did happen to me that summer. First, four of us from MBS' basketball team were invited to play in a summer league at a playground at 63rd and Lindbergh Boulevard in St. Barnabas parish. The games were on weekday mornings. So the four of us would meet early in the morning and walk about a mile and a half together to get to the playground.

The playground was in a peaceful neighborhood, compared to ours. To get to the playground, we'd walk along Kingsessing Avenue to 60th Street and head left toward Woodland Avenue. Then we headed right on Woodland Avenue, passing a part of the shopping area between 60th Street and 63rd Street. At this time of the morning, many workers were out in front of their stores, sweeping the sidewalk and talking with shoppers passing by. The whole atmosphere on Woodland Avenue had a peaceful feeling about it. There was none of the racial tension I could feel in the Chester Avenue shopping area in our neighborhood. Another big difference I always noticed was that hardly any of the stores along Woodland Avenue had the sliding, metal security gates that so many stores in our neighborhood had recently installed.

Once we got to 63rd and Woodland Avenue, we turned left and walked another half-mile to the playground on Lindbergh Boulevard. It felt so good to play basketball outdoors again. I don't think I'd played basketball outdoors in more than a year. When the games were over, we'd start our long walk back home, usually stopping along the way for some sodas and Tastykakes. As soon as we'd get close to our neighborhood, the easy part of our walk was over. It was time to start scanning the area ahead to make sure we took the safest route home.

The other cool thing that happened to me that summer was pretty amazing. One day, Mom got a phone call from Officer Tom McGlone. Tom told Mom that he was planning his annual three-week vacation to the Pocono Mountains, and that he was thinking about taking a group of us along to get us out of the neighborhood for a while.

He told Mom he wanted to take me, my brothers Joe and Larry, plus our friends Chris and Donny. Mom was thrilled, and so were we. But Mom was concerned about not having any extra money to send along with us. Tom told Mom he didn't want any money. He said he'd take care of everything. Mom couldn't thank Tom enough. She knew she'd miss us. But she also knew we'd be out of the neighborhood for three weeks. And that meant three less weeks she'd have to constantly worry about us. Mom's overworked nerves needed a break, too.

Officer McGlone had never married. It seemed to me that he was married to his job. He loved undercover police work, getting to know the kids in the gangs, trying to help them stay out of trouble, but making sure they paid the price when they started trouble. Because Tom worked undercover, he never wore a police uniform. And he never rode around in a police car. He always wore a white, short-sleeved, collared shirt with a tie. And he always drove up and down the streets of the neighborhood in a dark, unmarked sedan. Tom, more than any other adult, knew how dangerous our situation had become. He knew we were pretty much surrounded by black kids who now thought of the neighborhood as theirs, not ours. And they simply didn't want us around anymore.

So off we went, Tom and the five of us, squeezed into Tom's brand-new '72 AMC Gremlin, a car with a weird design that looked like a big section of the hatchback had been sliced off. The car's hatchback area and roof rack were jam-packed with our green plastic bags stuffed full of clothes for our three-week trip. After a three-hour drive, Tom pulled up to what would be our home for the next three weeks, a one-story cabin surrounded by woods on three sides. It was like we were in the middle of nowhere. I remember having a hard time sleeping the first few nights without the usual police sirens to lull me to sleep. But once I got used to the peace and quiet, I felt like I'd died and gone to heaven.

We had such a great time playing ball and hanging out at the mountain lake day after day without having to look over our shoulders to see if trouble was coming. At the lake, we made friends with a group of girls our age that let us ride around the mountain roads on their gas-powered mini-bikes. One day, when Chris and Donny were riding together on one of the girls' mini-bikes, they had trouble making a turn and smashed the mini-bike into a wooden post.

The post went down, but Chris and Donny and the mini-bike were fine. For the rest of our vacation, every time we'd drive by the fallen post in Tom's car, we'd all look at each other and flash a quick, secret smile. We didn't want Tom to find out what happened. And he never did. We had so much fun on that trip. It brought back memories of the days I roamed the streets of our neighborhood without a care in the world. Man, did I miss those days.

For three weeks, Tom took the five of us out to eat at least once or twice a day. We went to every kind of restaurant: American restaurants, Italian restaurants, Chinese restaurants, Japanese restaurants. I ate at more restaurants during those three weeks than I did the entire first 13 years of my life.

Every time we'd get into Tom's car to go out to eat or to go to the lake, Donny made sure he was in the front seat near the car radio. Donny had to control the music. He'd constantly hit the car radio buttons until he found his favorite song. That summer it was a song called "Alone Again (Naturally)." As soon as Donny found that song, he'd turn up the volume and start singing the words as loud as he could. And as soon as that song was over, DJ Donny would start hitting the buttons again, searching for "American Pie," his other favorite song that summer.

Tom must have spent a fortune on us. I couldn't believe he was doing this for us. He wanted us to have a great time, but he also kept us in line. Whenever one of us got out of line, by breaking something in the cabin or getting too rough fooling around, Tom would hit us with what we called a "short." He'd give whoever was out of line a short, powerful punch to the upper arm area that hurt like hell for a good five to 10 minutes. At one time or another, we all got hit with a few of Tom's short, powerful punches.

At night, we'd sit around with Tom, playing cards and talking about all kinds of things. We'd talk about some of the big games from past MBS football and basketball seasons. Tom would tell us some cool stories about police work. Plus, Tom would tell us over and over again how important it is that we do well in school.

I remember Tom saying, "If you want to live in a better neighborhood in the future, hit the books now."

One thing Tom never talked about was all the racial trouble in the neighborhood. I had a feeling he wanted us to forget about all that stuff for three weeks, so we could enjoy our time away. Plus, I think Tom wanted to forget about the neighborhood for a while, too.

That vacation was one of the best times of my life. But it went fast, way too fast. When we got back to Southwest Philly, it was mid-August, and the neighborhood felt even more dangerous than when we left, especially compared to all the peace and quiet we'd gotten used to in the mountains.

As summer came to an end, I was looking forward to all the guys getting back from the shore. And I was also looking forward to starting my first year in high school. What I didn't see coming was the dangerous situation I'd find myself in traveling back and forth to high school.

CHAPTER 17
September, 1972:
New School, New Danger

LITTLE DID I know at the time, but one of the best things to happen to me as a student ended up putting me in another dangerous situation. I was blessed to be a pretty good student. I usually had an "A" average. All the kids who were good students at MBS were urged to take tests for possible scholarships to private Catholic high schools in the Philly area. So I took the test for two schools.

A few weeks later I was stunned to find out that I got nearly a full scholarship to one of the city's best high schools, St. Joe's Prep, or "The Prep" as everyone called it. My parents were thrilled. And so was I, at first. It was a great honor to get a scholarship to a school like The Prep. But it also meant I wouldn't be going to West Catholic High School with all my friends, which I'd been looking forward to for years. I promised my parents I'd try The Prep for a year and see how it went.

Because The Prep was in North Philly, I had to travel in a completely different direction than my brother Joe and all my friends who were going to West Catholic. Those guys would meet every morning at 58th and Kingsessing Avenue to take the "G" bus together to West Catholic. About 15 to 20 of them traveled together, so they were safe in the mornings.

The "G" bus that took them to school traveled through a lot of black neighborhoods in West Philly on its way to West Catholic, which was in a black neighborhood at 49th and Chestnut Street. Along the way, their "G" bus would pass "G" buses going in the opposite direction that were packed with mostly black students heading to Bartram High School, which was in a white neighborhood at 67th and Elmwood Avenue.

It seemed strange that most of the white kids had to take buses to go to high school in a black neighborhood, while most of the black kids had to take buses to go to high school in a white neighborhood. "Forced busing" was another big issue that was constantly on the news. In some cities, the courts were forcing black kids to take buses to go to public schools in white neighborhoods, while forcing white kids to take buses to go to public schools in black neighborhoods. The courts said that forced busing was a good way to integrate the schools. Most parents, black and white, didn't like the idea at all. And many of those parents took to the streets protesting forced busing in their neighborhoods. Who could blame them? Why should some judge tell parents that their kids can't go to school in their own neighborhood?

The high school situation in our neighborhood had nothing to do with forced busing. The public high school, where most of the black kids went, just happened to be in a white neighborhood. And the Catholic high school, where most of the white kids went, just happened to be in a black neighborhood.

My friends who went to West Catholic were pretty safe every morning getting to school. And this year, even their trips home were much safer than the year before. Most kids from West Catholic rode home from school in special buses that waited right outside the school. Each bus took a different route, so every kid from every parish could get on a bus that would drop him off close to his house. The previous spring, when my brother Joe was a freshman at West Catholic, a lot of those buses were getting pummeled with rocks as they passed through certain black neighborhoods in West Philly. The same thing was happening to the buses headed home from West Catholic Girls High School, which was at 45th and Chestnut Street, just a half-mile away from the boys' school. As the buses continued to come under attack, the cops got involved. Since then, every bus returning from both West Catholic Boys and Girls High Schools had a cop car following right behind it.

My trip to high school every morning took me to a completely different part of Philly. The Prep was in North Philly, near 17th and Girard Avenue. So every morning, I'd walk to Chester Avenue to take the "13" trolley to City Hall. Then I'd take the Broad Street Subway up to North Philly.

The trip usually took about 45 minutes if the trolley and the subway were running close to schedule.

Every morning, as I waited for the trolley on Chester Avenue, a group of black kids my age would meet up right across the street from me. Then they would walk together to Shaw Junior High School, the public school near 55th and Warrington Avenue.

The black kids didn't mess with me in the mornings. A lot of mornings, Dad rode the "13" trolley with me to get to his day job at Penn Central Railroad at 33rd and Market Street. Even on the mornings when Dad wasn't with me, there were a lot of adults, black and white, waiting with me to take the trolley to work.

Still, even with all the adults around, sometimes the black kids would threaten me. The first time it happened, two black kids crossed Chester Avenue and stood right next to me. I had no idea what they were going to do. Then one of the kids said something to me just loud enough so only I could hear him, "We'll get you when you come home, when none of these people are around." And then the two kids walked back across Chester Avenue to join their friends.

I didn't see this coming. I had no idea going to The Prep was going to put me in this situation. One morning, they even threatened me when Dad was standing right next to me waiting for the trolley. Four black kids walked right across Chester Avenue, and came right up to me, right in front of Dad.

"Your daddy won't be with you when you come home," said Willie, the biggest of the black kids. "We'll get you then."

As I said, Dad's usually as easy-going as can be. But on that morning, he almost lost his cool. Dad's face turned beet red as he warned them, "You guys lay a hand on my son, and you'll regret it."

They were strong words coming from a man who tried to avoid confrontation whenever he could. I was proud that Dad said what he said. Unfortunately, Dad's warning didn't do much good. Lots of times Willie and his friends did wait for me. The nicer the weather, the greater the odds they'd be hanging out somewhere on Chester Avenue between 57th and 58th Streets, waiting for me to get off the trolley. So I always had to be on the lookout.

On every trip home, as soon as my trolley passed MBS Church at 56th and Chester Avenue, I'd stand up, grab the balance bar, and start scanning both sides of Chester Avenue. I had to quickly decide whether I'd be safer getting off the trolley at 57th Street or staying on until 58th Street. I had to get off at one stop or the other. And I had to make my decision even faster if no one else was getting off at 57th Street. If no one else was getting off there, I had to be the one to pull the cord above the window to let the trolley driver know someone was getting off at the next light. If no one pulled the cord and the light was green, the driver would keep going right through 57th Street to 58th Street.

As soon as my trolley passed MBS Church, the first thing I'd look for was a blue cop car. If I saw a cop car, my decision was made for me. I'd get off at the street closest to where the cop car was parked. If I didn't see a cop car, I'd look for Willie and his friends. If I saw them, I'd get off at the stop furthest away from them. Even if I didn't see Willie and his friends, I still had to assume they could be hiding out, waiting for me. It was like a game of cat and mouse. I had to guess where they might be waiting. They had to guess which street I'd get off at. Those times when the black kids guessed right, I either had to outrun them to my house or end up having to try to defend myself against the group of them until a cop or an adult in the area came over to help me out.

One afternoon, a black man about 40 years old helped me out. He was driving a Pepsi delivery truck that was stopped at a red light at 57th and Chester Avenue. When he saw that I was getting pushed around by Willie and three of his friends, he got out of the truck, and walked directly toward us.

"Hey, what's goin' on here?" he asked.

"Nuttin', sir," Willie said. "We just hangin'."

I didn't say a word. The man looked at me, and I could tell he knew what was going on.

"You leave this boy alone," he said. "Y'all hear me?"

"Yes, sir," Willie said, and the four of them started walking away.

"They bothering you?" the man asked me.

"They wait for me a lot when I get off the trolley," I replied.

"Well, you hurry on home now," he said.

"Thanks, sir," I said. "I appreciate what you did."

As I crossed Chester Avenue and headed home, walking as fast as I could without looking scared, the man got back in his Pepsi truck and drove away. Watching him drive away, I got to thinking about what my mom had been telling me and my brothers ever since our neighborhood started changing,

"There are good whites and good blacks. And there are bad whites and bad blacks." That man was definitely a good black.

A few days later, on my way home from The Prep, I finally got my opportunity to fight a kid that was a bad black, Duane. I'd always wanted to fight Duane for all the times he and his friends messed with us when we were outnumbered. And I wanted to fight him even more ever since the day he chased my younger brothers home from the grocery store.

On this particular afternoon, as soon as my trolley passed MBS Church, I got up, grabbed the balance bar, and took a look around. I immediately spotted a cop car parked near 58th Street, so that's where I got off. It was raining that day, not hard, but steady. I didn't see any black kids hanging out waiting for me. Sometimes even just a little rain made the streets a lot safer. I still walked home as fast as possible. When I was just two houses away from my house on Cecil Street, Duane jumped out from the alley up ahead near Kingsessing Avenue. He started running toward me, looking like he wanted to fight. I was all for it.

"Let's go, mother fucker," Duane said.

I looked around behind him to make sure he was alone. Then I said, "Right on. Let's go."

I put my books down on the sidewalk, I put my fists up in front of my face, and the fight was on, right in the middle of Cecil Street, right in front of my house. I figured it would be a fair fight, one-on-one, so I had no intention of taking my belt off and using it as a weapon. Even though Duane was about five-foot-11, a couple inches taller than me, he didn't weigh much more than I did. I thought I had a decent chance against him. So we started throwing punches. Duane hit me first, landing a roundhouse right to my left ear. Then I caught him good with a solid left to the right side of his face. After my punch landed, Duane reached into his coat pocket and pulled out one of those clear Bic pens.

"Oh shit," I thought to myself, "he's gonna try to stab me."

I blocked his first few tries with my left forearm. On his next try, my left foot suddenly gave way on a mix of rain and motor oil. The motor oil was probably from our neighbor Mr. O'Toole's old Studebaker. Because we didn't have a car, Mr. O'Toole usually parked his Studebaker right in front of our house when he came home from work. His car leaked oil all the time.

As soon as my left shoe made contact with the slick spot, my foot gave out from under me and I fell to the ground. Duane jumped on top of me, jabbing his pen into my back three times as I struggled to get back on my feet.

Just then, I heard our front door open and Mom yell, "Get the hell off him, Duane. Get out of here, you big punk."

Even Mom knew how much of a punk Duane was. Duane immediately got up off of me, took off running up Cecil Street, and headed back into the alley, like the snake that he was, going back into his hole. I was lucky I didn't get hurt from the pen. Unlike my friends who went to West Catholic, I had to wear a sport coat to The Prep every day. My sport coat took the brunt of Duane's stabs. It was the first time all year I was glad I had to wear that stupid coat to school. I didn't get cut at all, although I did have some puncture marks on my back where the pen jabbed me. Even though Duane got the best of me, I was happy I got one good punch in, something he could remember me by.

I didn't like going to school at The Prep. And it wasn't just because of the trouble I often had to deal with getting home. It had nothing to do with The Prep itself. The Prep was a great school with great teachers. I got good grades. And as the year wore on, I made some friends at The Prep. Ironically, a few of my closest friends at The Prep were black. I didn't like going to The Prep because I kept hearing how much fun all my friends were having at West Catholic. I missed being a part of it. It got to the point where I didn't even want to hear my brother Joe talk about all the fun they were having. I couldn't wait until the weekends, when I'd be back with the boys hanging out at MBS schoolyard, especially now that we'd started drinking beer.

CHAPTER 18
January, 1973:
Our Turn on the Front Lines

IT WAS THE same routine every Friday and Saturday night. We'd all meet up at MBS schoolyard around six o'clock. Because MBS gym wasn't open on weekend nights, we couldn't go into the gym to hang out and play basketball like we did during the week. We really had nothing to do on weekends except to hang out in the schoolyard. Only now, we started doing what our oldhead always did on weekend nights. We started drinking beer. We'd put all our money together to get a case of 16 oz. Schaefer cans, our favorite beer in our price range. Mom always gave me, Joe, and Larry a couple dollars to get a snack at the ice cream store near the schoolyard. Our ice cream money went directly into our beer collection.

As soon as we'd get enough money together, we'd ask one of the older Dirty Annies to get us beer. Most of the Dirty Annies weren't 21 yet. They either had fake IDs, or they knew where they could buy beer without an ID. For a couple months, one of the Dirty Annies was getting us beer in a taxi. He'd recently gotten a job driving a taxi a few nights a week. If he was working on a weekend night, he'd pull into MBS schoolyard in his taxi, and we'd pay him to get us some beer. It was pretty funny seeing him drive his taxi back into the schoolyard, knowing our beer was in the trunk.

While we waited for our beer to arrive, we'd gather the night's artillery. We were getting into street fights just about every weekend night. So we had to collect every bottle, rock, or any other potential weapon we could find. We'd usually hide our collection of weapons in a metal trashcan in a corner of the schoolyard next to Monsignor Dooley's garage.

Monsignor's garage was the first garage I ever saw with a door that went up and down by itself with the push of a button. The first time I saw it go up by itself, I couldn't believe my eyes. We didn't have many garages in our neighborhood. Most streets had just four garages, one at both ends of both sides of the street, usually right next to the alleys. Every garage I ever saw, except Monsignor's, had to be lifted up and lowered down by hand.

The metal trashcan near Monsignor's garage was a perfect place to hide our weapons. The cops couldn't see them when they'd drive by, and we could get to them right away when the fighting started.

When our beer arrived, we'd usually drink about two quarts of beer each in a back alley or on the front porch of a nearby row home where nobody lived anymore. In the past couple years, more and more houses were becoming abandoned as so many people moved out and so few people moved in. Years ago, there was hardly an empty house in the entire neighborhood.

When we finished drinking our beer, we'd walk back to the schoolyard to hang out. The beer definitely got us fired up for the fight that was likely to happen soon. As much as I enjoyed the buzz from the beer, I tried not to get too drunk. I knew I needed to have some of my wits about me when the fighting started. A lot of times, the guys who got really drunk got hurt the most.

One of our friends, Scott, was not a good drinker. Scott was a year younger than me. He'd drink just two cans of beer, and he'd already be slurring his words and having trouble standing up straight. Maybe it was because he was so young. Whatever the reason, one night Scott was really drunk when a fight broke out on Kingsessing Avenue. As soon as we heard some of the guys yelling that they were in a fight, we all headed for Monsignor's garage and grabbed whatever weapons we had hidden in the trashcan. Then we ran to the fight. When we got there, it was easy to see that we were outnumbered. So we tried to just hold our ground until the cops showed up. Bottles and rocks were flying. Belt buckles, broom handles, and car antennas were swinging.

Scott was so drunk, he didn't even realize how outnumbered we were. He just kept running straight ahead into the middle of all the black kids, swinging his belt in the air, yelling, "I'm gonna fuck you up!"

As soon as Scott said those words, one of the black kids whacked him across the ribs with a broom handle and down he went. We all tried to get to Scott's side, knowing if we could surround him we could protect him until he was able to get back on his feet. But there were too many black kids. We couldn't get past the first line of kids we were already fighting. Getting to Scott's side was impossible. They surrounded him and beat him up bad.

It reminded me of the way that black kid got beat up a few years ago by the Dirty Annies in front of our house. It had that same animalistic feel to it, like wolves attacking a fallen prey. Scott got pummeled with belts, broom handles, and kicks for about 20 seconds. That 20 seconds seemed like an eternity. All the while, out of the corner of my eye, I could see that Scott was getting beat up bad, but there was nothing I could do about it. I had to defend myself against the black kid I was fighting.

Finally, I heard the sounds I'd been waiting to hear, the screaming siren and screeching tires of a cop car making a high-speed turn up ahead at 55th Street onto Kingsessing Avenue. Right behind the cop car was a paddy wagon. Both were headed our way. The black kids ran down 56th Street toward Greenway Avenue. We stayed and gathered around Scott to see how he was. We knew that, by staying, there was a chance we could all get locked up. But we also knew the cops were more likely to go after the black kids because, this time, it was a white kid that got hurt. And that's exactly what the cops did. The cop car sped right past us and turned left on 56th Street to try to round up some of the black kids who were running that way. Had it been a black kid who got hurt, we would've been the ones running, and the cops would've been coming after us. I guess the cops figured that by rounding up some suspects right away, they could get a head start figuring out who was to blame if the injury turned out to be serious.

After the cop car sped by us, the paddy wagon came to a stop close to Scott, who was lying on the ground, moaning in pain. The two cops in the paddy wagon were able to get Scott onto a stretcher and into the back of the paddy wagon. Then they took off for the hospital. At that point, I figured it was better that Scott was so drunk. Maybe he wasn't feeling all the pain he was in. Scott ended up with some broken ribs and lots of cuts and bruises. Still, as bad as he got beat up, his injuries could've been much worse.

A lot of us were getting hurt in fights. The most common injuries were hits to the head or chest, usually from a belt buckle or broom handle. The worst injury I got was the night I got smacked across the head with a broom handle.

That night, the fight started when about 10 black kids attacked us, running at us from the Kingsessing Avenue entrance to MBS schoolyard. There were about 10 of us, too, hanging out in our usual spot on the steps of the annex building. Within seconds, the fight was on right there in the schoolyard.

I was in the middle of the pack; guys were fighting on my left and right. Luckily, I had my car antenna with me that night. On my first swing, I hit the black kid I was fighting across his right shoulder. I could see that I got him good, as he grabbed his right shoulder with his left hand.

My first reaction was to look to my right to see if any of my friends needed help. No one was in trouble on my right. Then I quickly looked to my left. All of a sudden I saw a fast-moving shadow coming from my right. A split second later, I saw stars.

Evidently, as I was looking to my left to see if any of my friends needed help, one of the black guys came over to help his friend, the kid I'd just hit with my car antenna. He caught me looking the other way, and he hit me square in the middle of my forehead with a broom handle.

"Help, I got hit," I yelled as loud as I could.

Two of my friends ran toward me, giving me some cover so I could get out of harm's way. As I backed away holding my head, I could hear the sirens of cop cars getting closer. We all ran toward Chester Avenue. I snuck away and sat on the steps of an abandoned house on Frazier Street to get off my feet and to get a sense of how bad I was hurt.

My head was throbbing. I could feel a lump the size of half a golf ball. Every time I pulled my hand away from my head, I expected to see blood. But I was lucky; it never bled. Unfortunately, my luck ended there.

Suddenly, a paddy wagon pulled up and stopped right in front of the abandoned house where I was sitting. The cop in the passenger seat got out, and started walking toward me.

"I got hit," I said, pointing to the lump on my head, which felt like it was getting bigger by the second. "My head's killing me."

I was hoping the cop would have some sympathy. He didn't.

"Get up and shut up," the cop said. "A couple of your friends are waiting for you."

After he handcuffed me, he opened the doors to the back of the paddy wagon. As soon as the doors opened, I saw that two of my friends, Billy and Ron, were already in there.

"Get in there with your friends," the cop said as he pushed me into the back of the paddy wagon and slammed the door shut.

Billy was yelling at the cop, "Let me the fuck out of here. We didn't do nothin'. I'm gonna sue your ass, McCluskey."

Officer McCluskey yelled back, "Shut the fuck up, Billy."

We knew all the cops' names. And they knew a lot of our names, as well. They all knew Billy's name. Ron didn't say a word to the cops. Last time Ron gave a cop some lip, the cop smacked him hard across the left side of his head with his huge walkie-talkie. That happened about a month earlier. Ron was still having a hard time hearing out of that ear.

That was the second time I got locked up. The cop who was driving the paddy wagon did the same thing as the cop who was driving the first time I got locked up. He kept slamming on the brakes, sending the three of us banging against the unpadded metal sides of the paddy wagon. Because we were in handcuffs, we couldn't even brace ourselves. The more we slammed into the sides of the paddy wagon, the louder the cops laughed.

After about 10 minutes of this, we finally arrived at the 12th District police station at 65th and Woodland Avenue. The cops put the three of us into the same holding cell. Four other white kids we didn't know were already in the cell. We knew we were only going to be in the cell for a few hours, but it was still a scary feeling when those thick, steel bars slammed shut in front of us. As we were sitting in the cell, the cops marched four of the black kids we were fighting right past our cell and into another holding cell right next to ours. The trash talking began.

"Honky mother-fuckers, we'll get y'all tomorrow night," one of the black kids yelled.

To which Billy yelled back, "Fuck you, nigger."

The taunting continued back and forth until a cop walked past both holding cells, banging his nightstick against the jail bars and telling us all to "shut the fuck up."

Because we were all under 18, we knew the cops would call our parents and tell them to come pick us up. The cops decided whose parents would be called in what order. So it was a good idea not to mouth off to the cops. The guys who gave the cops a lot of lip sometimes stayed in jail three or four hours longer than everybody else. Billy was the last one out of jail that night.

Because my parents didn't have a car, and we lived more than a mile from the police station, Mom had to call a neighbor to ask for a ride to get one of her boys out of jail. Dad was bartending. It made for an awkward ride home. I didn't say a word. And neither did Mom. I knew she was upset.

But she seemed to be getting used to this, now that me and my two brothers had already been locked up a total of six or seven times. When Mom would get the phone call from the cops, I actually think she was relieved when she found out we were in jail, not in the hospital, or worse.

Every weekend in the schoolyard, the street fights were getting more frequent and more violent. It was getting out of control. One Friday night, a fight broke out in the middle of Chester Avenue that, in my mind, brought this whole crazy situation full circle.

When we all squared off to fight, I was shocked to see that I was matched up with Dwight, the black kid I was friends with years earlier when we played basketball together. I hadn't seen Dwight in months. Both of us had our belts off. We looked at each other as if to say, "This is really crazy." In Dwight's eyes, I saw the eyes of a friend, a friend like my brothers, like Chris, like Donny. Was I supposed to try to hurt Dwight because he happened to be hanging out with the black kids we were fighting? Just like when we used to play basketball together, we both knew what to do without saying a word. We both began swinging our belts toward each other. I could tell Dwight wasn't trying to hit me. And I didn't want to hit him, either. But we both knew we had to make it look to our friends like we were trying to hit each other.

All the while, I was hoping the cops would show up soon. They did. And we all scattered. Me, Chris, and my brother Joe ran through some alleys and ended up on 56th Street near Springfield Avenue. We quickly hid behind some overgrown hedges on the front lawn of a row home, hoping we could stay there until things settled down.

Evidently, the cops saw us. Two cop cars pulled up in front of the house where we were hiding. A cop in the lead car pointed the car's blinding search light right at us. The three of us got up from behind the hedges with our hands in the air, and climbed out onto the sidewalk. That's when I noticed that there was also an unmarked car behind the two cop cars. It was Officer Tom McGlone's car. When Tom realized it was us, three of the kids he had taken on vacation the previous summer, he told the other cops that he knew who we were, and that he'd take care of the situation.

Tom took one look at us and I could tell he knew we'd been drinking. I'm sure he wasn't happy about that. But I sensed he wasn't mad at us for fighting. Tom knew us well enough to know that all this fighting wasn't something we wanted to do. It was something we had to do. He knew MBS schoolyard was the only territory we had left in the whole neighborhood. And we had no other choice but to defend it. Tom told us to get in his car, and he drove us home.

CHAPTER 19
February, 1973:
Agnes, Our Angel

I'D KNOWN AGNES for about a year. I first met her one night at Cahill's Tavern. Dad was bartending, and I was bringing him a sandwich from home. It was one of those nights when Dad didn't have time to come home to eat. He'd get off the trolley from his day job and walk directly to Cahill's to start his night job. As soon as I walked into Cahill's through the ladies' entrance on Alden Street, I saw Agnes sitting alone with her mixed drink at one of the wooden tables in the back of the bar. I said hello as I sat down at a table next to hers. Little did I know what a huge impact this tiny Irish lady, who looked to be in her seventies, would have on our family's future.

Agnes was a pretty lady, although she wore a bit too much blush, which really stood out against her pale complexion and crop of short, white hair. Dad told us about Agnes a few weeks earlier. He told us this nice older lady had recently started coming into Cahill's on the nights he was bartending. Agnes lived a short walk from Cahill's, on Chester Avenue, just eight or nine row homes down from the bar.

In the year that I'd known Agnes, I could tell she really liked my dad. She'd always tell me, "Kevin, in all my days, yur dad's the nicest bartender I've ever come across."

Agnes once told Dad she felt that some of the other bartenders at Cahill's didn't like having her in the bar. She told Dad they made her feel like she was bothering them. She could tell they didn't like having to leave the bar area, which was nearly always crowded, just to wait on her in the ladies' section in the back of the bar. So Agnes usually only came to Cahill's on nights Dad bartended.

Dad didn't mind waiting on Agnes at all. He went out of his way to treat her special. That's one of the things I've always admired most about Dad. He always tried to make everybody feel special. He went out of his way to be nice to people. He gave the same respect to the man who emptied our garbage can in the back alley as he did to the cop walking the beat on Chester Avenue. He was the same way with us five boys. He made all five of us feel special. I never got the feeling that any one of us was his favorite.

So it never surprised me that so many people liked Dad. I was always impressed with the genuine smiles that brightened so many people's faces whenever they'd run into Dad on the street. Everybody knew him. I guess, sooner or later, bartenders in neighborhoods like ours get to know just about everybody.

On the nights I brought Dad a sandwich while he was bartending, he would give me a couple glasses of ginger ale and a pack of crackers. As I sat in the back of the bar enjoying my snack, Dad would sneak away from the bar every chance he'd get to sit down with me and take a few bites of his sandwich. On many of those nights, Agnes would be sitting at a table near mine, alone with her drink. She always tried to start a conversation with me. She seemed genuinely interested in getting to know me. She'd ask how school was going, did I like to play sports, did I have any girlfriends, questions like that. Sometimes Agnes would talk about how bad the neighborhood was getting. I could tell Agnes was upset about it. She told me she was really upset when she found out that me and my two brothers were with Doug just minutes before he was killed.

One night, Agnes said to me in her broken-Irish accent, "Kevin, I keep tellin' yur dad he should move you and yur brutters out of this God-forsaken neighborhood."

"Yeah, Agnes," I said, "it's getting crazy out there."

I knew how much Dad wanted to move. I also knew we didn't have the money to move unless we were able to sell our house. And that didn't look like it was going to happen anytime soon. But I wasn't going to tell Agnes we didn't have the money to move. And I knew Dad had way too much pride to tell her. Evidently, Agnes figured it out for herself. One night, when Dad brought Agnes' drink back to her table, she asked Dad if he had a minute to talk. Dad said he did, and he sat down with her. Agnes told Dad that she had some money saved, and that she wanted to lend him some to help us move out of the neighborhood.

I heard about it the next night. My parents were talking in the kitchen. I was eavesdropping, which was way too easy to do in our tiny row home. When Dad told Mom what Agnes said, Mom was thrilled.

"Joe, we have to do this," I heard her say. "These kids are in danger."

"Then let's do it," Dad said.

Right on, I thought to myself, we might be moving! By now, I was definitely ready to move. As much as I loved this neighborhood, it was nothing like it used to be. The danger now far outweighed the fun. Finally, I could allow myself to think that, someday soon, we might be moving to a safer place. I tried to never think about it in the past because I didn't want to be disappointed. But now, at last, there was a good chance it was actually going to happen.

When Mom and Dad told me and my brothers that we might be moving, I never saw a group of happier kids. A few days later, Mom took the five of us to Agnes' house so we could thank her. Agnes let us into her home, which she shared with her sister. Her sister looked a lot like Agnes. She also wore a bit too much blush. She seemed nice, but not nearly as friendly as Agnes. After we thanked Agnes, she told us how happy she was to be able to help. In my mind, she was an angel sent down from God!

The following Saturday morning, Mom asked me to go with her to look at some houses. When the realtor drove up to our house, we got in the car and off we went. Joe stayed home to watch our younger brothers. Dad had bartended the night before, so he was catching up on some sleep. Besides, Dad didn't really care where we moved. He had just three requirements. First, the house had to be in move-in condition. Dad never used a tool in his life, so there was no way he wanted to move into a house that needed lots of work. Second, because we didn't have a car, the house had to be in walking distance to public transportation. Third, the house also had to be in walking distance to a bar. That's not to say that Dad liked hanging out in bars. He didn't like it at all. I think he got his fill of bars on the nights he bartended. Dad wanted a bar nearby so he could stop in on his way home from work and pick up a six-pack of beer. Because Dad worked so much, he liked to spend as much of his free time as possible at home with me and my four brothers. He still enjoyed his beers, but he enjoyed them at home, watching sports with us on TV, especially Dad's beloved Phillies, and especially when Dad's favorite Phillie, Steve Carlton, was pitching.

Dad was a huge Steve Carlton fan. The previous summer, Dad took one of us with him to just about every home game Carlton pitched. I couldn't wait for my turn to go with him. Ever since Veterans Stadium opened in 1971, we could just ride the "G" bus to the game. The trip was so much easier than having to travel up to Connie Mack Stadium in North Philly. To get to Veterans Stadium, we'd take the "G" bus to the end of the line in South Philly. Then we'd walk over to the stadium, which was about a mile and a half away. Dad loved to walk, and he walked fast. I always had a hard time keeping up with him. After the game, Dad would stop at the ticket window and buy two cheap seats for the next game Carlton was scheduled to pitch. The tickets were easy to get because the Phillies were awful that summer. They played 156 games, and they only won 59 of them. But here's the amazing part. Of the 59 games they won, Carlton won 27 of them! He was the best left-handed pitcher I ever saw. His slider made even the best hitters look silly. It was no surprise that Carlton won the National League Cy Young Award that went to the year's best pitcher. To win 27 games with that team, he certainly deserved that award. He was incredible.

Anyway, where was I? Oh yeah … finding a house. On our first day house hunting, me and Mom looked at houses in Northeast Philly. Lots of our friends whose fathers were Philly cops and firemen had already moved to the Northeast. They had to keep living in the city if they wanted to keep their city jobs. The following weekend, we looked at houses in the Delaware County suburbs. Literally hundreds of families from MBS had already moved into safer suburbs like Yeadon, Darby, Upper Darby, and Lansdowne.

I definitely wanted to move to Delaware County for one reason: it would be quicker and safer for us to get back to Southwest Philly. Me, Joe, and Larry had already talked about coming back to the neighborhood on weekends after we moved. If we moved to Delaware County, we knew we could get a bus to 65th and Greenway Avenue, which was just a half-hour walk from where our friends were hanging out. If we moved to the Northeast, it would take us twice as long to get back to the neighborhood. Plus we'd have to travel through some bad parts of the city.

We convinced Mom that Delaware County was our best choice. Of course, we didn't tell her why. The last thing she needed to hear was that me and my brothers were already making plans to come back to Southwest Philly on weekends.

On the day me and Mom looked at houses in Delaware County, we found a perfect twin house in Havertown that met all three of Dad's requirements. It was in move-in condition. It was a three-minute walk to the bus. And it was a two-minute walk to the bar. Dad loved it. We made settlement on the house in late April, but Mom didn't want to move in until June so Larry could graduate eighth grade at MBS.

A few weeks after we made settlement on the house, Dad told us that Agnes hadn't been in Cahill's for a couple weeks. When Dad ran into Agnes' sister on Chester Avenue, he asked her if Agnes was OK. She told Dad that Agnes was in the hospital with pneumonia. A few days later, on a night Dad was bartending, Agnes' sister walked into Cahill's through the ladies' entrance. When Dad saw her, he knew something was wrong. He'd never seen Agnes' sister in Cahill's before. Dad walked back to see her, and she told Dad some bad news. Agnes died in the hospital. It was sad to hear such bad news about such a good person. I wished I knew more about Agnes. I wished I knew more about the generous person who was about to make such a huge difference in our lives. But I guess she'll remain a mystery. She reminded me of the guardian angel from that Jimmy Stewart movie, *It's a Wonderful Life*. Agnes did her good deed for us, and just like that, she was gone.

One day, less than a week after Agnes died, I answered our phone. Agnes' sister was on the line, and she asked to talk to Mom or Dad. My first thought was that she might be demanding the money back that her sister had lent Dad. But it turned out to be just the opposite. She told Mom that, after Agnes lent us the money, she changed her will. Dad didn't have to pay back the $3,000 Agnes had lent him. When Mom told me what Agnes' sister said, all I could think was, "Agnes really was our angel!"

CHAPTER 20
June 6, 1973:
Only Three More Days

STILL TRYING TO *catch my breath, I continue walking up Cecil Street to our house. I take a quick look back to Chester Avenue to make sure there's no sign of Willie and his friends who were chasing me. Right on! The coast is clear. Maybe the cop nabbed them. I hope so. For a change, I can actually walk home at a normal pace without having to constantly look over my shoulder.*

"Just three more days," I keep reminding myself, "and we're moving out!" I take a slow, long look across the public church's grounds over to Myers playground. I'll definitely miss Myers playground. As bad as things got over there, the good times I had in that playground far outweigh the bad.

Then I take a look at all the houses up and down Cecil Street. I used to know everybody who lived on this street. And they all knew me. Now, I don't know half the people who live here. Most of the new families are black. The few black neighbors that I've met seem nice. Most of the white people who still live here are trying to move out. There are six "For Sale" signs on our street, including ours. As I look at our "For Sale" sign sticking out of our tiny garden, I remember all the fun we had in that house when we were kids. But then my mind quickly flashes back to all the danger we faced living in that house in recent years. Every time I look at our front porch, I can still see Mom getting punched in the face through the screen door. No, I won't miss that house at all.

Then I think to myself, "How did this neighborhood ever get so dangerous?" And I really don't know the answer. It's easy to say that when black people started moving in, the neighborhood started getting dangerous. So should I just jump to the conclusion that all the trouble was the black people's fault? What about the fact that both the whites and the blacks started their share of trouble? What about all the black friends I made over the years at school in MBS, playing sports at Myers playground, and at The Prep? Once again, I'm reminded of Mom's words, "There are good whites and good blacks. And there are bad whites and bad blacks."

Then I wonder if other factors were involved, other than race. Why did the realtors keep calling white families to try to get them to move? Was it greed, so they could sell more houses and make more money no matter what impact it had on our neighborhood? Why did so many white families move out, even before a lot of the serious trouble started? Was it to protect their investments in their homes, or was it fear of what they thought living here would be like if they stayed? And why did so many black families move into our neighborhood? Was it part of some inner-city population shift? Obviously, I've got a lot more questions than answers.

One answer I do have is based on something I learned in my studies this year at The Prep: the struggle for territory nearly always leads to violence. In our neighborhood the past few years, there was definitely a struggle for territory. The battles in Myers playground, in Myers gym, in Cobbs Creek Park, in MBS schoolyard, throughout the whole neighborhood really, were just as much a struggle for territory as many of the battles in the wars I studied at The Prep. In a way, even the constant shoulder-to-shoulder bumps on the sidewalks were a struggle for territory, neither side willing to give up even one inch of ground. Hopefully, the longer I go to school, the more sense I'll be able to make out of some of the stuff that happened around here.

Another thing I definitely learned is that we have to play the hand we're dealt in life. We had no control over the fact that the neighborhood we lived in got so dangerous, so fast. But we couldn't let the danger lead to fear. No, we had to find ways to reduce the danger: like protecting ourselves with belts and car antennas, like factoring in the weather when deciding which route to walk, like changing walking routes to avoid becoming too predictable, like constantly scanning everything going on around us to avoid trouble as much as we could.

The most important lesson I learned, I learned from Dad. Dad taught me how important it is to treat people the right way. After all, without Dad's kindness toward Agnes, we wouldn't be moving out of this neighborhood in three more days. It's that simple.

As excited as I am to be moving out, I feel bad about leaving behind guys like Chris and Donny who still have to live here. Both of their families are trying to move out, too. I hope they do. At least I know I'll be back hanging out with them on weekends. And I also know this: no matter what happens in my life after we move, I'll never forget the guys I went through this experience with. I have a strong feeling that the bonds we formed living through these dangerous years together will remain with us for the rest of our lives.

EPILOGUE
Looking Back

ON THE FIRST FEW YEARS AFTER WE MOVED:

As we anticipated, Joe, Larry, and I did come back to Southwest Philly on most weekends the summer after we moved and for the better part of the next two years. The summer after we moved, MBS schoolyard was simply too dangerous for our friends to hang out there anymore. So they started hanging out on the west side of Myers playground, along Kingsessing Avenue, between 59th and 60th Streets, which was still a mostly white area. That location was perfect for my brothers and me. The bus we took from Delaware County dropped us off at 65th and Greenway Avenue, just a 15-minute walk from where our friends were now hanging out.

Myers playground had become a buffer zone, almost two blocks wide, which separated the whites on one side from the blacks on the other. We still got into street fights, but not nearly as often as we did when we were surrounded by black kids in our final days hanging out in MBS schoolyard. It was great to be back, hanging out in the old neighborhood every weekend. And the best part was: we didn't have to take that dangerous walk home to Cecil Street every night. Cecil Street was on the black side of the Myers playground buffer zone. So a big part of the danger we faced when we lived on Cecil Street had been eliminated.

I never did go back to St. Joe's Prep. And I never went to West Catholic, either. When we moved to Havertown, my brother Joe and I both transferred to Cardinal O'Hara High School in Springfield. My brother Larry went to Haverford High School for one year, then he joined Joe and me at O'Hara.

Toward the end of my junior year in high school, I started hanging out on weekends with O'Hara friends I'd gotten to know playing basketball. So my weekend trips back to Southwest Philly became few and far between. Still, I kept in touch with a lot of the guys from the old neighborhood, and I got together with some of my closest friends as often as I could.

ON SELLING OUR HOUSE ON CECIL STREET:

Our house remained unsold for another two years after we moved. We never did find a buyer. Mom and Dad simply sold it to the realtor for $3,000 just to get it off their hands. During those two years when our house was empty, we still kept one bed in the house. Dad wanted to keep working his second job bartending at Cahill's for as long as possible. On the nights Dad bartended, he'd sleep in our empty house. Then, in the morning, he'd take the "13" trolley back to his full-time job at Penn Central Railroad.

Considering how long it took us to finally sell our house, Agnes' financial help was even more crucial. We would have been stuck, living in those dangerous conditions for at least a couple more years. Who knows what would have happened? I'm sure I would have had at least a few more chapters to write.

ON BEING SCARED:

When our neighborhood got so dangerous, I admit I was scared at times. We all were. Now that I don't *have* to be scared anymore, I don't *want* to be scared anymore. You'll never catch me watching a scary movie or reading a scary book, ever.

ON SOME OF MY FAVORITE BASKETBALL PLAYERS WHEN I WAS GROWING UP:

Back in Chapter 4, I described Joe Bryant as one of the up-and-coming high school stars everyone was talking about in the Myers Playground Summer League. Joe Bryant did become a star at Bartram High School. Then he played three years at LaSalle University before entering the NBA draft. Joe played for the 76ers for the first four years of his eight-year NBA career. He also played professionally for seven years in Italy. Along the way, Joe got married and had two daughters and a son. His son's name is Kobe. He plays professional basketball, too. You may have heard of him.

Also in Chapter 4, I mentioned that Richie Berberian was my favorite basketball player in the Myers Summer League. Richie was a great player at West Catholic High School and at Hiram Scott College. As I pointed out in the book, Richie was a terrific guy. A lot of us younger guys got to know Richie during the summers when he worked at Myers playground. After Richie got out of college, he joined the Air Force Reserve where he came down with a rare muscle disease. He died from that disease in 1972. He was only in his early twenties. I couldn't believe a guy so young and healthy could die just like that. I'm just glad I got to know Richie the short time he was here.

If you remember from Chapter 15, Michael Brooks was one of the black kids from MBS parish who played basketball with us in MBS gym. He was the best player then, and he kept getting better. As a senior at West Catholic, Michael was named 1st Team All-Catholic and led his team to the Catholic League Championship Game. After high school, Michael, like Joe Bryant, decided to stay in Philly and play college basketball at LaSalle, where he had a spectacular career. As a senior, Michael was a consensus 1st Team All-American, the Big Five Player of the Year, and the ninth player selected in the first round of the NBA draft. Michael went on to play six years in the NBA with the Los Angeles Clippers, Indiana Pacers, and Denver Nuggets. He then played professional basketball in France for eight more years.

ON RUNNING UP BILLS AT THE LOCAL STORES:

Mom and Dad's financial situation would have been even worse if stores back in the sixties and seventies operated the way they do today. Nowadays, Mom and Dad would have had to pay by credit card, which means they would have had to pay interest on top of interest on all the IOUs we racked up in the old neighborhood. Back then, the storeowners who extended credit didn't charge Mom, or anyone, even one penny of interest. They simply extended credit as a courtesy to families in the community that needed help to make ends meet. And I know, at least in our family's case, their kindness created a lot of repeat business for their stores.

ON MY REUNION WITH DWIGHT'S BROTHER, LONNY:

Evidently, the excitement of working on the school newspaper at MBS remained in my blood. After graduating from Cardinal O'Hara High School, I majored in journalism at Temple University in North Philly, which I commuted to from my parents' house in Havertown.

During my second year at Temple, the father of one my best friends from high school helped me get a full-time job at *The Philadelphia Inquirer*. My friend's father was an executive at *The Inquirer*. He knew I wanted to get into the newspaper business. So he helped me get a job working the four-to-midnight shift in *The Inquirer's* Advertising Art Department.

My job required that I spend a lot of time on the Composing Room floor, where the pages of the newspaper were pasted together. One night, on the Composting Room floor, I saw a young black guy that I'd never seen there before. He was about my age, in his early twenties. I kept looking at him. I knew his face. But I couldn't remember who he was. Then it hit me. It was Dwight's brother, Lonny. When I went over to introduce myself, Lonny remembered me. He asked how my brothers were doing. And I asked him about Dwight. Lonny said Dwight was doing well, which was great to hear. Lonny had just been hired at *The Inquirer*. Whenever I saw Lonny, we'd stop and talk about sports, about work, and about our families. The one thing we never talked about was all the racial trouble back in the old days. I could sense that, for both of us, it was a subject we wanted to leave in the past. I know that's how it was for me.

ON MY MOVE BACK TO THE OLD NEIGHBORHOOD, SORT OF:

When I started my job at *The Inquirer*, I was still living in Havertown with my parents. Every morning, I'd drive into the city and park my car in a lot near *The Inquirer*, which was near Broad and Vine Streets. Then I'd take a 10-minute ride on the Broad Street Subway up to Temple University in North Philly. When classes were over, I'd take the subway back to *The Inquirer*, get a bite to eat in the employee cafeteria, sign in at four, and work until midnight. Between college and work, I was spending so much time in the city, I decided to rent an apartment in the city with one of my good friends from our old neighborhood, Ron. Ron was the kid who got hit in the head with the cop's walkie-talkie. To this day, Ron still has trouble hearing out of his one ear.

When Ron and I talked about where we wanted to rent, we both agreed we wanted to be as close to the old neighborhood as possible without being in harm's way. That way, we would be close to a lot of our old friends who were still living in safer sections of Southwest Philly. So we rented an apartment at 45th and Kingsessing Avenue, just over a mile from where we grew up. At the time, in 1979, 45th and Kingsessing Avenue was on the outskirts of University City, the ever-expanding area of West Philly near the University of Pennsylvania and Drexel University. University City was a racially diverse area with a mix of college students, young business professionals, and some black families who'd probably been living in the neighborhood for decades. I remember thinking that the black families who lived there for so long were finally getting a break. For the first time in decades, their property values were actually going *up*, not down. Good for them. It was so refreshing to live in an area where white people and black people lived side by side without violence, without name-calling, without even staring each other down.

Whenever I would visit some of my old friends in Southwest Philly, I'd drive along Kingsessing Avenue straight through the heart of our old neighborhood. As I'd drive by, lots of black kids were usually hanging out on the corners, not a white face to be seen anywhere. Every time I'd drive by Cecil Street, I'd glance down the street to try to catch a quick glimpse of our old house. What an advantage it was to be able to just drive past the gangs of black kids, instead of having to sneak around them like we had to do in the old days.

ON THE ONE MODERN CONVENIENCE I WISH WE HAD BACK THEN:

If I could go back to those dangerous years and have just one modern convenience we have today, my decision would be easy. I'd want a cell phone. With cell phones, we would've been able to let each other know where the trouble spots were. Plus, we could've called for help when we were in trouble. I have no doubt cell phones would have helped us avoid a lot of danger.

Just as important, cell phones would have helped make Mom's life a lot less worrisome. If we had cell phones back then, Mom would have been able to keep in contact with us when we were hanging out on the streets. As a parent myself, I can't imagine not having cell phone communication with my two kids. And my kids grew up in a safe neighborhood. I don't know how any parents back then, white or black, were able to relax knowing their kids were hanging out in that neighborhood night after night with no communication at all. I don't think they ever did relax until their kids returned home safe and sound.

ON THE VIETNAM WAR:

Thank God, the Vietnam war ended in 1973, three years before I would have been eligible for the draft. I definitely didn't want to have to spend a night watching the draft lottery, petrified that those ping pong balls bouncing around in that big drum could play a part in how long I might live. After the war was over, I still wasn't sure whether we won or lost. It wasn't until I saw the movie *Stripes* in 1981 that I finally got the answer. In this military comedy, actor Bill Murray becomes the leader of a group of social misfits going through basic training. While trying to fire up his trainees, Murray proudly says *"... we're American soldiers. We've been kickin' ass for 200 years. We're 10 and one."* I'm pretty sure the "one" he was referring to was the Vietnam war. So from that point on, I figured we lost that war.

ON THE OLD NEIGHBORHOOD TODAY:

Over the years, I've seen a lot of stories on television and in the newspapers about our old neighborhood. Nearly all of the stories were negative. It's been the scene of numerous murders, many of them drug-related gang shootings.

The last time I drove through our old neighborhood was back in 1996, when I took my two young children there to show them where I grew up. They'd been asking me to show them for a while. Because the old neighborhood was so dangerous, I wanted to take them at a time when I thought there'd be as few people as possible on the streets. So I decided to take them early one Saturday morning around six o'clock. I was usually up early with the kids, anyway. My son, Christian, was six years old at the time. My daughter, Jenny-kate, was just four. Both kids fell sound asleep on the 45-minute ride from our home in West Chester to Southwest Philly. When we got close to our old house, I tried to wake both kids. My daughter wouldn't budge. But my son woke up. As soon as he realized where we were, he pressed his face up against the car window. At least half of the homes we drove by were now boarded up.

The first words out of my six-year-old son's mouth were, "Dad, didn't you have any paper when you were growing up?"

I couldn't figure out what he was talking about, so I asked him, "What do you mean?"

He replied, "Why does everybody write on the walls? Don't they have any paper?"

I couldn't help but laugh at my six-year-old son's reaction to all the graffiti spray-painted on virtually every inch of every wall everywhere we looked. When we drove down Cecil Street to see our old house, I stopped to get my camera ready so I could take a quick picture. Wouldn't you know, the moment I was ready to take a picture, a black teenager walks out the front door of our old house onto the front porch. This kid looked to be about 17 years old, and he looked like he just woke up. So the first thing this kid sees, as he's wiping the sleep from his eyes, is a 38-year-old white guy in an SUV with two young kids in the back seat. And the white guy is pointing a camera at him. I'm sure the kid didn't know what to think. And there was no way I was going to stick around and try to explain it to him. So I quickly snapped a picture of our old house with the kid standing on the porch, and I drove toward Chester Avenue.

At Chester Avenue, I made a right turn toward MBS schoolyard. All the entrances leading into the schoolyard were padlocked shut. The chain-link fence surrounding the schoolyard was now topped with a layer of barbed wire. Near the schoolyard, many houses and storefronts were boarded up. Lots of cars were abandoned. And trash was piled up on empty lots where houses once stood. It was sad to see. When I left the schoolyard area, I decided to drive past Myers playground and head back home to West Chester.

ON MYERS PLAYGROUND:

As I slowly drove along the Chester Avenue side of Myers playground, I could see graffiti spray-painted on every wall. Also, the playground now had a big in-ground swimming pool, which was built shortly after we moved out of the neighborhood. Other than the graffiti and the pool, everything else in the playground looked pretty much the same as it looked back in the early seventies. Driving past Myers playground that day, I got choked up a bit as I thought about all the great times we had in that playground. It was my favorite place in the world for a lot of years.

Nearly 10 years after my trip back to the old neighborhood, in 2005, I was reminded once again of all the great years we had at Myers playground. It was my son's first year playing high school basketball. He was playing in a summer basketball league in a playground in Narberth, a small town just outside the City Line Avenue border of West Philly. I'd never been to the Narberth playground before. On this comfortable April night, my wife and I took our son to his first game. As we walked into the playground, I immediately felt an eerie sense that I'd been in this playground before. The more I looked around, it suddenly dawned on me: Narberth playground in 2005 was Myers playground in 1969. For the first time in more than 30 years, I felt that unmistakable sense of community togetherness that I hadn't felt since the old days at Myers playground. Just like at Myers playground, it seemed as if the whole neighborhood had flocked to Narberth playground for the evening. Just like at Myers, young kids, with their parents looking on, played on the swings and sliding boards. Just like at Myers, two little league baseball games were under way at the same time, while players' parents watched from metal bleachers behind chain-link backstops that extended down the first- and third-base lines. Just like at Myers, there was a room tucked inside an old stone building that sold water ice and pretzels. And, just like at Myers back in the day, the main focus was on the basketball courts, as many of the best high school players in the area went head-to-head in the best summer league in the area.

A few weeks later, my son's team was playing in a late game at Narberth playground. By the time the game was over, darkness had already settled in. As we walked across the playground to the side street where our car was parked, I saw something that stopped me in my tracks. There, in another corner of Narberth playground, just like at Myers playground, neighbors of all ages were setting up blankets and lawn chairs, getting ready to watch an outdoor movie. When I saw that, I stopped and took a long look around the entire playground. I wanted to soak it all in. It felt so good to experience, once again, the magical way a great playground can bring an entire community together, the way Myers playground once brought our old neighborhood together, and the way Narberth playground was now bringing its neighborhood together.

ON MOST BLESSED SACRAMENT (MBS) PARISH:

MBS School closed for good in 2002. At the time, MBS had only 150 students in the entire school. Remember, this is the same school that had nearly 3,500 kids back in the sixties.

MBS Church remained open for another six years. Then, in 2008, after 117 years, MBS Church closed its doors for good. But this glorious structure still stands, the crucifixes on its palatial green domes still looking down over the entire neighborhood. The church in the basement is still in use, serving as a thrift shop. The inside of the upstairs church has been gutted. Many of the church's magnificent artifacts and stained-glass windows have been removed and were incorporated into the renovation of a church in Holland, Pennsylvania, St. Bede the Venerable.

MBS school buildings are now home to the Hardy Williams Academy Charter School. MBS convent now serves as a women's shelter. And MBS rectory is now being used by a group of nuns who still do social work in the community.

As you might expect from an inner-city school that once had almost 3,500 kids, the letters "MBS" continue to be a source of pride for generations of people throughout the Philly area. I'm constantly amazed at how many people I run into who either went to MBS themselves, whose parents went to MBS, or whose grandparents went to MBS. They're everywhere!

ON DAD, WHO CAME TO BE KNOWN AS "JP":

As my brothers and I got older, Dad became less of a father and more of a sixth brother. In fact, we didn't even call him "Dad" anymore. We called him "JP." JP was always hanging out with his five boys and our friends: drinking beers, watching sports, and playing pinochle. JP loved being around us, and we loved having JP around.

One year, JP actually got to spend some time with his favorite Phillie of all time. It was the night of the 1994 Major League Baseball All-Star Game. JP's favorite Phillie, Steve Carlton, then retired, was a guest at a casino in Atlantic City. He was there to sign autographs for casino customers before the All-Star Game got under way.

At that time, a friend of our family, named Larry Mullin, was in a management position at the casino. Larry liked JP a lot, and he knew how much JP liked Steve Carlton. So Larry invited JP to come to the casino to meet Carlton. Two of my brothers, Steven and Larry, picked up JP and drove him to Atlantic City. They ended up in a big reception room where casino customers were lined up to meet Carlton. JP kept saying, "C'mon, let's get in line before the game starts." JP knew that Carlton was only going to sign autographs until the opening pitch of the All-Star Game.

My brother Steven said, "JP, Larry said we should wait here."

As game time approached, JP could see that Carlton was getting ready to leave. Now JP was getting nervous. "I think he's leaving," JP said. "Let me just go and shake his hand."

Steven repeated, "Trust me, JP, just wait here."

JP watched anxiously as Carlton left the room and got into an elevator. As soon as Carlton disappeared into the elevator, our friend Larry Mullin came into the room where JP and my brothers were waiting. Larry walked up to JP and said, "C'mon, JP, you're coming with me."

Larry led JP and my two brothers to the same elevator Carlton had just gotten on. When they got off the elevator, Larry led them into a private suite, and there, enjoying some fine wine, was Steve Carlton, along with Phillies catcher Darren Daulton and retired Phillies pitcher, Larry Christenson. For the next hour, JP was hanging out and enjoying some drinks with his favorite athlete, Steve Carlton. From what I heard, Carlton and JP hit it off pretty well. A casino photographer came into the room and took some pictures of Carlton with his arm around JP. JP was on cloud nine for weeks. He was so proud to show everybody the pictures of the time he was hanging out with Steve Carlton. Later that summer, my brother Steven took JP up to Cooperstown, New York, so he could be there in person to see his long-time idol and new friend, Steve Carlton, inducted into the Baseball Hall of Fame.

Dad hanging out with Steve Carlton at Atlantic City Casino.
From left: Larry Mullin, Steve Carlton, and Dad.

After leading an extremely healthy life, JP was diagnosed with lung cancer in 1995, at age 66. The prognosis was not good. We were told to expect his death soon. But JP fought hard, and with the help of a great doctor and some effective chemotherapy, JP made a remarkable comeback. His comeback enabled him to be out on the dance floor at the wedding of our youngest brother, Steven. So JP ultimately lived to see all five of his sons get married. When JP's cancer went into remission, we made sure we spent as much time with him as we could. One day, we rented a stretch limo and took JP and his brother, Uncle Jim, to see a baseball game at the new, state-of-the-art baseball field in Baltimore. It was JP's first ride in a limo, and we had a great day. Shortly after that trip, the cancer returned, followed by a stroke. JP died in June of 1997.

At JP's viewing, so many people lined West Chester Pike that the funeral home had to stay open an hour and a half later than planned. Some of my friends told me they had to wait in line for more than two hours, which is quite a tribute to quite a man!

ON UNCLE WALT:

At about the same time Dad was battling cancer, Uncle Walt was battling Alzheimer's disease. Uncle Walt was living in the rectory at a Catholic Church in Augusta, Georgia, where he had served as pastor for many years. On Valentine's Day, 1999, we got a call that Uncle Walt had died suddenly of a heart attack. Given the years of dementia Uncle Walt faced, his heart attack was probably a blessing. Mom, my brothers, and I flew down to Augusta for his viewing and funeral. The church was packed both days. Following his death, the parish named a building after him, calling it "Fr. Walter L. DiFrancesco Parish Center & Gymnasium."

As I mentioned in Chapter 13, Uncle Walt was extremely thrifty. As a priest, he didn't have many expenses, yet he was paid a modest salary all those years. Evidently, he saved a lot of his salary. Before Uncle Walt's funeral, we were going through his belongings, looking for any keepsakes that we wanted shipped back home to us. As we were going through his stuff, one of Uncle Walt's most trusted friends came into the room and handed Uncle Walt's financial files to my oldest brother, Joe. After quickly reviewing the files, Joe walked over to my Mom and said, "Mom, you don't have to worry about money anymore." Uncle Walt left all his money to Mom. It wasn't a fortune, but it was enough money that Mom won't have to "rob Peter to pay Paul" for a long, long time to come.

ON MOM:

With Dad and Uncle Walt passing away within two years of each other, Mom had suddenly lost the two most important men in her life.

When Dad got sick, we could see that Mom was wearing down from the stress of having to take care of Dad's medical needs day and night. We began to worry about Mom's health. After Dad died, Mom seemed to relax a bit. But I think, in the back of her mind, she knew she might ultimately end up having to take care of her brother, Uncle Walt, who was gradually losing his struggle with Alzheimer's disease. After Uncle Walt died, I could sense all the weight being lifted off Mom's shoulders. As time went by, I could see in Mom's face that she was finally learning to relax. For the first time I can remember, she didn't have to worry about taking care of everybody else, as she had for so many years. All the stress Mom had to endure, raising five boys during those dangerous years in Southwest Philly, was becoming a distant memory. These days, it's so nice to see Mom enjoying herself, sharing so many good times with her sons, her daughters-in-law, and especially her 12 grandchildren. No one deserves it more!

ON MY BROTHERS:

Every summer, during the last week of June, well into the early hours of the morning, on a second-floor deck overlooking the surf in Ocean City, New Jersey, you'll hear lots of laughter coming from my four brothers and me as we play game after game of pinochle, while drinking bottle after bottle of beer. It's become an annual tradition for our families to vacation together every summer. And we have an absolute blast. It's easily my favorite week of the year.

We started the tradition once we all started having kids. Four of us have two children; Marty has four. Getting everybody together for that week has helped mold five small families into one big family, like the really big families from our Southwest Philly neighborhood. Sometimes, when all 12 of our kids are eating at the long dining room table at our vacation house, I think about some of the parents from our old neighborhood that had to feed 12 kids or more every day in their tiny row homes. No wonder so many families had to eat in shifts.

Because all four of my brothers still live in the Philly area, we get together as often as we can for birthdays, holidays, Eagles games, Phillies games, Sixers games, any excuse we can find. I thank God we made it out of the old neighborhood without criminal records, and without any of us getting seriously hurt. Over the years, all five of us have been promoted into management positions in our chosen fields of business. Throughout my life, I've gotten to know lots of families with a lot of kids, but I've never come across a group of five brothers that are any closer than the five of us. And I pray we'll remain that way.

ON WHY I THINK THE NEIGHBORHOOD GOT SO BAD, SO FAST:

During the mid-to-late sixties, a lot of black families that were already living in dangerous neighborhoods were looking to move into safer neighborhoods. At that time, our neighborhood definitely qualified as a safer alternative. So a lot of black families moved in. If that influx of black families could have happened at its own natural pace, I think the change could have occurred in a much more peaceful manner. Sure, there would have been some trouble. After all, the sixties were racially explosive years. Sadly, some of the realtors took advantage of that racial tension. As I said in the book, many realtors flooded the phone lines night after night, trying to drum up fear among working-class white families, so they could sell more houses and make more money. The realtors' tactics worked. Droves of white families moved out. And who could blame them? For many working-class families in our neighborhood, their home was their biggest, and often their only, investment. So, when the realtors convinced them that their biggest investment was at risk, many white homeowners did what they thought was best. They sold their homes, usually to black families, leading to a sudden, drastic racial turnover that never had even the slightest opportunity to slowly and naturally evolve at its own pace. The result was an immediate struggle for territory on the streets, which, in turn, led to so much violence and, ultimately, the needless loss of life.

ON GROWING UP IN A RACIAL BATTLEGROUND:

I wouldn't trade my childhood with anyone else's, anywhere. I got to experience both ends of the spectrum: unbridled joy as a child and unbelievable danger as a young teenager. We grew up fast. We had to. In a very short period of time, we were transformed from a group of young kids playing sports all day into an inner-city gang having to protect ourselves and our territory. Through it all, we developed a sense of loyalty and togetherness most kids our age never experience. We were ready to fight for each other anytime, anywhere. Plus, we gained a sense of perspective that would serve us all later in life. Whenever tough times come, as they inevitably do, I think back to those dangerous years in our old neighborhood and say to myself, "Things could be a lot worse."

As proud as I am to have grown up in that neighborhood, there's no way I would have wanted my children to have to live through what we lived through. As a parent, I wouldn't have been able to handle the stress. I don't know how our parents did it. I guess they simply had no other choice.

ON THE GUYS FROM THE OLD NEIGHBORHOOD:

More than 40 years later, the bonds among the guys from our old neighborhood are as strong today as I'd thought they'd be, perhaps even stronger. Some of the guys from the neighborhood are still some of my best friends. Some I talk to once or twice a week. Some I talk to once or twice a month. Others I talk to once or twice a year. I still see a lot of the guys at parties, weddings, graduations, funerals, and summer barbeques.

Whenever we get together and talk about the old days, the conversation usually ends with words to the effect of, "Man, those days were crazy, weren't they?"

Yeah, those days were crazy. But those days forged special bonds among us that we continue to share to this day. We still feel a sense of loyalty to each other that, I suspect, is similar to the way many war veterans feel about the guys they fought with. And why shouldn't we feel that way? After all, at a very young age, we fought together on the front lines in a Philly war zone.

Edwards Brothers, Inc.
Thorofare, NJ USA
January 24, 2012